Successfully Managing
Your Accounting Career

THE WILEY/RONALD-NATIONAL ASSOCIATION OF ACCOUNTANTS
PROFESSIONAL BOOK SERIES

Jack Fox · *Starting and Building Your Own Accounting Business*

Denis W. Day · *How to Cut Business Travel Costs*

Gerald M. Ward and Jonathan D. Harris · *Managing Computer Risk: A Guide for the Policymaker*

Harry L. Brown · *Design and Maintenance of Accounting Manuals*

Gordon V. Smith · *Corporate Valuation: A Business and Professional Guide*

Harvey L. Shuster · *The Financial Manager's Guide to Microsoftware*

Henry Labus · *Successfully Managing Your Accounting Career*

Successfully Managing Your Accounting Career

HENRY LABUS

JOHN WILEY & SONS
New York · Chichester · Brisbane · Toronto · Singapore

To my wife, Mary Jo,
the "best planned" person I know

Library of Congress Cataloging-in-Publication Data:

Labus, Henry.
    Successfully managing your accounting career / Henry Labus.
        p.   cm. — (The Wiley/Ronald-National Association of
    Accountants professional book series)
    Bibliography: p.
    ISBN 0-471-63388-7
    1. Accounting—United States—Vocational guidance. 2. Career
development—United States. I. Title. II. Series.
HF5616.U5L23   1988
657'.023'73—dc19   88-14871
                                                              CIP

Printed in the United States of America

10 9 8 7 6 5 4 3 2 1

PREFACE

The past two decades can accurately be described as a time of explosive change in the accounting field. Evidence of this phenomenon is most profound in the computer revolution, the growing number of corporate mergers and acquisitions, constant changes in the federal tax laws, and the vulnerability of the CPA profession to lawsuits by clients. These changes have complicated the life and career of the accountant. In the next two decades, the influence of Japanese management techniques, the successful assimilation of minority accountants into the field, and changes in the quality of work life will result in a new and more demanding role for modern accountants. This role wil require a better balance of personality and technical skills to survive the demands of a constantly changing business world.

Accountants will go through an average of five job changes during their career. Approximately 40 percent will not be too happy with their jobs. How will accountants handle the trauma of being passed over for promotion or being fired? How do accountants plan, when their career has reached a plateau? How will they handle working for the new breed of accountant, five to ten years junior in age, or for a nonaccountant executive transferred in from out of town? How do accountants handle a job and a divorce simultaneously?

Most colleges do an excellent job of teaching future accountants the technical skills necessary for finding a position in their field. Once college is completed, however, neophytes are left to fend for themselves. College curriculum administrators have not yet recognized the great need for practical career planning courses that will steer accountants wisely through their career years and into retirement.

This book addresses that need. It recommends practical ways of developing a flexible career-maintenance plan that considers the major obstacles that may arise. I have drawn upon 30 years of successful accounting, recruiting, and career planning experience, including counseling with hundreds of corporations and several thousand accountants, many of them members of the National Association of Accountants.

Although this book was written for accountants about planning an accounting career, I am dedicating it to my wife, Mary Jo, who is not an accountant. For thirty-five years I have observed and admired her creativity as a teacher and in planning her teaching career. I also want to give credit to the National Association of Accountants, which opened the door for me to develop skills in writing, communication, and career planning. Without this help, I would find it difficult to write on this important and timely subject.

HENRY LABUS

Detroit, Michigan
August 1988

CONTENTS

1. Career Planning—A Lost Art   **1**

The Cloudy Future of Promotions   2
Slenderization   3
The Battlefield of Business   3
Avoiding Extinction and Slippage   4
Reactive Planning   4
The Tragedy of Erroneous Planning   6
Basis for Game Plan   6

2. Balancing Home and Career Life   **9**

Quality of Work Life   9
The Hop Performer   13
Mastering the Art of Conflict   13
Divorce: A Fact of Life   16
A Job: Also a Fact of Life   17

3. Mastering the Art of Competing   **21**

Match Your Style with Company Culture   22
You Can't Compete with a Coronary   23
Expect Some Stress—It Can Help You Compete   25
What You Can Do to Minimize Stress in your
Subordinates   33

If Stress Already Is Your Problem, Reverse It   34
Live Positive Thinking   35
Learn to Cope with Your Boss   38
Learn to Cope with a Younger Boss   42
Learn to Cope with an Older Boss   43
What Your Boss Expects of You   44
Are You Power Driven?   50

4. **Taking Charge of Smart Time**   **55**

Identify Your Most Productive Time   55
Schedule "Smart Time" for Decision Making   57
Utilize Visualization Techniques   59
Develop Work Habits That Will Last a Lifetime   63
The Problem Solver   73
Motivation   78
Need for Self-Esteem   79

5. **When You Have Reached a Plateau**   **87**

An Acceptable Plateau   91
An Unacceptable Plateau   92
Plan of Action   95

6. **Designated Annual Career Planning Day—Your
    Birthday**   **109**

Update Your Résumé Annually   110
Discuss Your Personal Development With Your
Manager   110
Hold Your Résumé in Abeyance   112
Review the Previous Year   112
Plan for Your Next Birthday   115

7. **To Change or Not to Change—That Is the Question**   **119**

When Should You Seriously Consider a Job
Change?   120
How To Resign with Class   127
Midlife Crises (Changes in Life)   135
What to Do When Your Company Is Acquired   137

8. **Career Changes**   **141**

Entrepreneurship   143

Sales and Marketing   153
Consulting   155
Public Accounting   157

9.   **Ethical Considerations**   **159**

Nice Guys Can Finish First   160
Moral Commitments   162
Establishing a Standard of Integrity   162

10.   **Changing Currents in the Accounting Field**   **165**

Effect on Undergraduate Education   166
Effect on Graduate Education (MBAs, MSTs, and Other
Degrees)   167

11.   **Greater Demand for Continuing Education**   **169**

A Wider Field of Competition   169
Changing Tax Laws   169
Upgrading of Skills (CMA, CPA, CIA, CFA)   170
Communication Improvement Courses   170
Computer Courses   173
Job Enrichment Courses   174
Build Your Library to Reinforce Your Game Plan   179

12.   **Membership in Professional Associations**   **183**

AICPA: American Institute of Certified Public
Accountants   184
NAA: National Association of Accountants   184
AAA: American Accounting Association   186
IIA: Institute of Internal Auditors   186
AFP: Accredited Financial Planner   186
CFP: Certified Financial Planner   187

13.   **Public, Private, and Teaching Careers**   **189**

Public Accounting as a Career   189
Private Accounting as a Career   192
Teaching as a Career   194
Moonlighting   197
Planning for Retirement   201

14. Conclusion   205
     References   207
     Index   209

1

CAREER PLANNING—
A LOST ART

Strange as it may seem, most accountants know very little about developing and maintaining a realistic career plan for themselves. Those who lack written goals that are measurable and attainable are forever condemned to work for those who have such goals. I have come to this conclusion after interviewing and counseling over 3,000 accountants and financial executives in the past decade.

Approximately 90 percent of those interviewed had only a sketchy idea of their career's long-range direction. Only about 10 percent had a definite, documented plan of their future expectations. This is amazing. We invest four long years of our precious time and thousands of dollars for schooling in preparing ourselves for a 40-year career. Once we attain the career, however, all we do is occasionally make sketchy mental notes of what we plan to do with it. My recent sojourns in local libraries and bookstores confirmed my suspicions that their shelves were filled with the wrong books for this purpose. Popular subjects such as how to get hired, writing better résumés, and interviewing techniques abounded. But I could not find a single book on career planning or maintenance, to guide professionals through those treacherous 40 years on the job.

There seems to be a parallel between our careers and the way we take care of our personal health. We reluctantly decide to see doctors only when we feel sick or we are in pain. But a physical checkup every year would put us in much better shape and could add years to our lives, assuming we followed our doctors' advice. The same goes for career plans. We would certainly have a better chance to attain our goals if, once a year, we reviewed and analyzed our performance and accomplishments, and revised or updated our job plans. These plans would definitely be more meaningful if they were detailed in writing or recorded on tape. By documenting these plans in some regular manner, we can evaluate our progress, analyze any shortcomings that have developed, and make necessary adjustments. But this type of thinking, though it makes a great deal of sense, has become a lost art. I hope to revive it in this book.

☐ THE CLOUDY FUTURE OF PROMOTIONS

The U.S. Bureau of Labor Research estimates there will be 1.2 million practicing accountants by 1995. Many of us still believe in a magical business world in which, if we find the right accounting job and work very hard, everything will fall into place. Not so. This plan worked well for Dad's generation, but it simply won't work for us today. We must take the time to plan and become responsible for mapping our own career, because no one else will.

By the year 2000, roughly 17 percent of American job holders may be working at home using a computer screen. Telecommunications will be the province of the professionals, if employers can only get over their fear that unsupervised workers will work less productively at home. Demographers foresee a decade that will spawn large groups of frustrated employees with thwarted goals. They anticipate large-scale job-hopping and scarce promotions over the next 10 to 20 years. Take the plight of the 45-year-old chief financial officer (CFO) at a large Pittsburgh hospital. He couldn't adjust to a new computer system that promised to release him from his number-crunching tasks to do more meaningful analytical work. He clung to his trusted adding machine until he was fired and replaced by a younger, computer-literate manager.

The new breed of accountants, the post–World War II babies, are better educated, more skilled, and more affluent than their elders. Their personal, material, and social interests tend to be more important to them than job loyalty or security. This shift reflects broad social trends. The "womb-to-tomb" concept of work is dead, and few employees today are willing to "walk on hot coals" for their companies. They believe employment is not a privilege, but a right. They are simply not too concerned about what track their careers will take in the future; they are concerned with the present, and their interest in long-range career planning is in a holding pattern.

☐ SLENDERIZATION

Corporate giants like General Motors, Ford Motor Company, and Unisys (Burroughs/Sperry) have publicized plans for management "slenderization" and white-collar reduction during the late 1980s. Nationwide, similar events have worsened the current relationship between middle managers and their employees. Larry Hirschhorn, senior manager at Wharton's School of Applied Research, University of Pennsylvania, says, "Basically, I think people no longer have confidence in companies or believe that they can make a lifelong career. It's a less stable world out there." Since 1979, middle management has been reduced by 15 percent worldwide, a percentage that will definitely increase considerably in the next decade. Generally, people do not have confidence in corporations, or believe companies can offer them secure careers. The instability of the world and its economics influences this kind of thinking. The role of middle management has been eroding in recent years, and will continue in that direction in the next decade.

☐ THE BATTLEFIELD OF BUSINESS

The business world today is beginning to resemble a battlefield. It is in such a state of flux that accountants, in self-defense, must do a much better job of monitoring and feeling the pulse of their careers than in the past. They are doing battle in the midst of a minefield of major obstacles that may arise throughout an accounting career. They must learn how to move through the minefield to reach their objective safely. Unless they can locate individual mines, their lives will be threatened. Once they detect the mines' locations, they must carefully detonate each mine without exploding it. Only then will they have safe passage. The following chapters show how to locate these mines and how to detonate them safely.

□ AVOIDING EXTINCTION AND SLIPPAGE

Scientists claim that one reason that dinosaurs vanished from the earth was the tendency for their bodies to grow faster than their brains could adapt. Career slippage develops when an individual does not adapt to important changes in the professions.

Few of us realize that good career planning, initiated early and administered properly, can be utilized as a powerful way to keep us from heading toward extinction. Career extinction is possible for any of us, if we do not stay current with the times.

A worthwhile strategic plan should contain a reasonable balance among ourselves, our employer, and our families, and one other ingredient—lifetime self-improvement courses. The trade-offs we decide to make will determine whether our strongest pull will be toward our company or for our personal life. Thus a future plan is born.

□ REACTIVE PLANNING

Most of us engage in "reactive planning": we wait until significant events happen in our lives before we get excited enough to do any serious planning. Examples are not hard to find.

1. *Lack of promotion:* Accountants tend to drift into jobs that sound good but offer few promotional opportunities, challenges,

or satisfying assignments. Only when we have been passed over for promotion do we begin a hasty reevaluation of our career path and start thinking negatively about our future with the company. Rumors of an imminent merger or acquisition may also trigger renewed attention to our future promotion possibilities.

2. *Loss of job:* Nothing accelerates career planning faster than being fired, quitting, or seeing the handwriting on the wall. But it's harder to plan your career strategy when you are under heavy pressure and your concentration is focused mainly on obtaining another position or defending the present one.

If there is a hell on earth, its ultimate punishment must be to wake up one morning with nowhere to go, nothing to do, no more challenge to set our hearts pounding. Work adds dignity and purpose to life. Without it, we are terribly diminished.

3. *Need for more income:* How many times have I heard excited applicants who have just become proud parents tell me they need a better paying job—one with more responsibilities—and *quick.* Suddenly they are serious about career advancement.

4. *Divorce:* Divorce often prompts career swings and takes a heavy toll on the quality of work. The by-products are job loss, transfers, and demotions. The emotions involved are the main factor here. Our 1986 studies show that about 40 percent of our applicants for jobs have been divorced in the previous two years. For recently divorced accountants, career planning usually goes on the back burner.

5. *Midlife crises:* This often misunderstood phenomenon usually occurs in people between the ages of 45 and 55. Their careers may have peaked with their job dreams still unrealized. They may have lost one or both parents in recent years. Psychologically, they are depressed and confused—and the job becomes the culprit. They no longer have strong family buffers to fall back on. At this late stage, they begin thinking seriously about changing careers. Our 1984 telephone surveys of 30 companies show that a disappointingly small number of companies have any policies on this subject.

6. *Acquiring a professional designation (CPA, CMA, CIA, MBA, etc.):* How often have you heard an accountant announce

proudly, "Once I get my CPA, I'll have it made"? The CPA designation is the golden passport to the executive washroom, and the open door to power. The new CPAs' evaluation of their career potential zooms to new heights. Their strategy now takes on a new meaning and a new direction. Should they ask for a raise? Remain in public accounting and shoot for a partnership, or go private? Which could be more rewarding? Should they rethink their career plan?

The MBA or its equivalent, in my opinion, is only valid for ten years. Beyond that, it self-destructs because of the fast changes occurring in business every decade.

All these types of reactive planning lead to patchwork career solutions, which may not pass the test of time.

☐ THE TRAGEDY OF ERRONEOUS PLANNING

Career planning should be an accountant's top priority. The most unforgettable accountant I have ever met was a Big Eight CPA who literally had his career explode in his face. "Bob Switzer," a married man with two children, considered himself a failure at age 40. It will be very difficult for me to forget the fixed, angry look in his eyes as I reviewed his career status with him. It was clear that his career meant everything to him. And his career progress seemed fine. As vice-president for finance of a small manufacturing company, he had a fine career ahead of him, but his own perception was a dismal and negative one. A short time later he committed suicide. His life must have been hell on earth for him.

☐ BASIS FOR A GAME PLAN

Sooner or later you will question your choice of accounting as a permanent career. Hundreds of our firm's applicants have experienced such second thoughts. This is a normal reaction when one's career is at a crossroads. Fortunately for these applicants, their dormant careers were steered in a direction that suited them. As a rising financial executive on my way up the unstable ladder, I also experienced doubts about accounting as my permament career. In two decades as an accountant, I progressed from the inexperience of a junior accountant to the uncertainty of a senior accountant, and then to the excitement as well as the frustration of the plant, division, and corporate controller. I made a career change at an appropriate time in my life. For 15 years I have reviewed probably every conceivable career problem. From this foundation, I will discuss career guidance and maintenance plans that can reward you for the rest of your working days.

2

BALANCING HOME AND CAREER LIFE

Our culture worships comfort. It is almost impossible for accountants to make realistic and successful career plans without taking into consideration their home life objectives and needs for comfort.

☐ QUALITY OF WORK LIFE

The workplace has undergone sweeping changes in the past two decades. The quality of work life accountants embrace will definitely determine how fast they move up the changing corporate ladder—if they move up at all. Assuming they work 8 hours a day and drive 1.5 hours to and from work, typical accountants spend 47.5 hours or 42 percent of their waking hours on the job. That leaves 64.5 waking hours a week, or 58 percent, quality time available for family life or personal pleasure. (We assume 56 hours a week of nonquality, but necessary, sleep time. How we plan to use those 112 waking hours (assuming we have the right education, experience, and attitude) is important. To take control of our lives, we must determine to a great extent our relative commitment to work and to personal life.

9

Although modern managers accept that quality of life is a desire of the new breed of professionals, they do so reluctantly. Commitment to quality of life weakens employees' devotion to the company's needs and to the work ethic itself. Ideally, management would prefer to call the shots in directing subordinates to produce the best work output possible. But managers lose part of this control when employees are influenced by a new interest in quality of work life.

A professional working parent will be hard pressed to give 100 percent to a job. It takes a tremendous amount of concentration, dedication, and isolation. For people who do give 100 percent of their time to work, all the other elements of personal life are diminished. There is simply not enough time or energy left for other pursuits.

Job Preservation Needs Sacrifice

Webster's New World Dictionary of the American Language appropriately describes *sacrifice* as "foregoing of some valued thing for the sake of something of greater value." So it goes with job security. If we value our job, what's wrong with making some sacrifices? Job security is what we make of it. We cannot count on the company taking care of us if we work hard. We must learn to take care of ourselves and be prepared should our job be terminated.

Early in my career as assistant corporate controller of a manufacturing firm, I was "asked" to work Saturdays. The treasurer wanted to keep his budget performance looking favorable, so he assigned two salaried executives to substitute for two clerical workers who would have had to be paid overtime. After many Saturdays of mundane clerical work, I developed enough nerve to confront my superior and politely advise him of the "unfair" treatment. To my surprise, he responded angrily, "If you don't like it, leave." There is an important lesson here. I reasoned that it was more important to keep my job by continuing to be a team player than to rock the boat then and there. I stayed. My response followed the accepted logic of the times: "no gain without pain." Today's rising executives, however, influenced by a mania for instant gratification, might handle this dilemma differently. They probably would not consider the long-term effect of their decision, and they might quit. Today's executives find it increasingly difficult to give the company quality time that is reserved for family or personal activities.

Job Demands Need Family Input

I urge accountants to begin to discuss quality of work life with their families. No matter whether you are 30 or 50 years old, whether or not you have ever talked about this subject with your family before, this is a good time to start. Who knows your ambitions and dreams better than your spouse? Who knows more about your assets and attitude toward your job than your family? You have to decide how to plan your career within the framework of your combined life-styles. Decide together whether family or career should come first, or whether to try for a balance of both. When you have your family's backing, they will be supportive of your career plan from the beginning.

How Much Overtime Is Right?

The average middle management executive works about 45 hours a week. Upper management financial executives spend at least 55 hours a week on the job. Chief executives, who work 60–70-hour weeks and give up many of their weekends and their family relationships, do put their careers first. The heads of 1,300 of the largest U.S. corporations accept their rigorous work routines as necessary, and are willing to pay the price. If you are determined to move into a top echelon position, and you have accurately assessed your qualifications and possibilities, then you had better plan to add more productive time to your work schedule. Obviously, then, you must subtract some of your leisure time. Some of your overtime should be targeted for improving your rapport with your superiors or peers. Your competition is certain to put in their necessary extra time.

Will You Travel for the Company?

A typical management accounting position may involve at least 10 percent travel time for the rising executive. Before you discuss potential travel with your family, first determine whether your partner and/or children can *handle* your being away from home for long periods of time. Turning down assignments that require extended travel will definitely hurt your career, but it will not actually put your job in jeopardy.

Business travel has its disadvantages, too. Many auditors' careers have been ruined or stalled as a result of indiscriminate use of leisure time while on business trips. A certain amount of temptation is inherent in this type of travel. Auditors, after all, are the experts from out of town, the official representatives of the home office. Sometimes they are viewed with fear and suspicion. Reports of any abnormal behavior on their part can easily filter back to the home office or to the family, where they may cause problems. Travel is one of the top time-wasters in business.

Loyalty and Discipline Can Be Revived

Loyalty is not just an old-fashioned, out-of-date concept. It is, however, somewhat misdirected, and is not used as much today in the office as it should be or as it was in earlier years. In 1964 I became a controller for the first time. My employer was a small manufacturing firm. I was thrilled, and I gave the job everything. I even slipped in to work on Saturdays without the CFO's knowledge. Real honest-to-goodness loyalty was deeply ingrained in my psyche, along with a fear of not growing with the company. I believe it came with the territory of the times. The training and discipline I had learned in three years on U.S. Navy antisubmarine duty had fostered this mental attitude. Many younger accountants have not had an opportunity to develop this kind of discipline in the armed services. Sports participation, too, develops team spirit or allegiance. Strong family ties are another way of experiencing loyalty. Loyalty is a natural characteristic, one we all have, ready to tap when desired. Show me one executive who would not prefer subordinates to exhibit a certain amount of loyalty on the job.

☐ THE HOP PERFORMER

Your peers and friends may admire you for your ability to manipulate home, office, and play at the same time. Concentrating, balancing, focusing, and being flexible—all characteristics of the peak HOP (home–office–play) performer—require talent and, most of all, planning. If you don't know what you want out of your career, you will never have enough time to juggle three equally important things at the same time.

☐ MASTERING THE ART OF CONFLICT

Resign Yourself to Job Conflict

Any job that doesn't involve conflict or pressure isn't much of a job. Every job I have ever worked on as an accountant has had its associated share of conflict and stress. As professionals, we must resign ourselves to the fact that we are destined to work with such conflict for our entire work lives. Then we can actually anticipate job conflict and learn to manage it. Those of us who are lucky or smart enough to have learned how to love our jobs may even crave conflict in order to enjoy solving the problems that arise. How many times has your CFO given you a hot assignment when you felt there was not enough time to do the job adequately? Even if you let him know, the deadline may still stand—perhaps because of a set date for the next board of directors meeting. You complete the assignment by taking work home and working through several lunches; you solve the potential conflict through personal and family sacrifice.

The president of a consumer products manufacturer, having difficulty understanding the complexity of computers, once advised me (as controller) to fire or "get rid of" the entire 19-person computer department. He said the computer was of no use to the company because the computer printout erroneously showed 3,200 cases of a particular widget in inventory. The president went out to the warehouse and, on his hands and knees, counted the inventory. You guessed it—he counted 4,000 cases. The pressure was on me. I did not respond immediately. For one day—until he cooled off—I made myself scarce. The next day, he was receptive to a rational explanation. We were on a dual electronic data processing (EDP) system because we were upgrading the old system. The president had inadvertently obtained the old printout, which was one day old.

I thought that was my last day on the job. Remember—you can take any situation you're in and make it work for you.

The Dual-Career Family

Gone are the days when the husband was the sole breadwinner, leaving the wife to supervise the family. With a growing number of two-income families, employees also are demanding more time off from the job, contributing to more employer–employee conflict. The affluent, two-career family must juggle heavy work demands with family pressures—a child's sickness or the threat of a babysitter canceling. As more women take advantage of improved career opportunities, either partner's job may suffer. When a third party is managing the children, there are more phone calls and more stress. Corporate executives are beginning to recognize that anything employees do outside the company is going to affect the quality of job performance. Still, companies are primarily interested in what accountants can do for them productively, and on the company's terms, despite any family problems. Accept home–office conflict as a part of life, and do your best to solve each conflict as it occurs. Learn to roll with the punches. Know your strengths, take advantage of them, and be willing to make sacrifices when the company beckons.

Allocating Time

If you are part of a two-career family, you should set your priorities as follows:

1. Evaluate your and your spouse's available free time and determine how best to manage it. Friction often arises over whose needs come first.

2. Estimate whose time will be utilized on certain work days for home emergencies. If you are a controller and your wife has an equally important job, it may not be obvious whose time is most important for the family as a whole, but be sure you hear your spouse's opinion—it may not agree with yours. In a household where two careers compete for room, bruised feelings are often brushed aside amid the tumult of other domestic changes. Suddenly, the intrusive evening and weekend phone calls from the office are for *her*.

3. If you jointly consider the spouse's job as more important (salary-wise), the situation must be treated differently, and delicately. My wife, Mary Jo, and I have a dual-career marriage. She is devoted to the schoolchildren at Harding School in Ferndale, Michigan, where she has taught first grade for 34 years. She spends countless extra hours on special projects for her classroom, just as I do for my company. We consider our two careers equally important, and we share equally in household chores.

Relocation: How It Affects Home Relationships

Before deciding to accept a new position or a transfer that involves pulling up stakes, consider the following questions:

1. Is the new salary worth moving to Timbuctu? Is this really a promotion, with potential, or just a lateral move? If the latter, it may be wise to consider turning down the transfer.

2. If a wife is being transferred and will earn more money in the new job, will her husband be supportive and cooperative in the move?

3. Does the new job become more permanent and secure in the long run? This is important, because problems will usually crop up at home as a result of any relocation.

☐ DIVORCE: A FACT OF LIFE

As professionals, we must accept the phenomenon of divorce as a fact of business life. Divorce affects every human endeavor in corporate life—and the accounting and finance departments are no exceptions. You may be one of the divorce statistics; your assistant or your boss may be another. The more you know about the psychological effects of divorce on corporate and home life, the better prepared you will be to handle them. You must learn to recognize the symptoms of an impending divorce and the aftereffects of an actual divorce in the lives of any of your subordinates.

Sudden Change in Work Habits

Employees may suddenly develop atypical work habits or exhibit excessive signs of emotion or frustration. Usually such employees will confide their personal problems to close associates, and in time the news will get back to the boss. Telltale signs include excessive absenteeism, a lackadaisical attitude, excessive errors, and abnormal emotional behavior.

What do you do when you become aware of such emotional problems?

1. Plan a humane approach to the problem. It is very real and very serious to the employee, who definitely does not realize any change has occurred in personality or attitude. One of my assistants, when going through a divorce, told me that her husband was so angry he punched a hole in the closet door. She definitely felt better after telling someone about it.
2. Try to listen sincerely in an attempt to help deflate the pent-up emotion.
3. Tell employees you support and sympathize with them, but emphasize that they must do their share to control their emotions during work hours.
4. Keep personal discussions private—behind closed doors, if possible.

5. If, after continuous warnings, nothing seems to help, you might suggest a leave of absence or an early vacation, or even recommend professional counseling.

6. Finally, as a last resort, if the disturbance is absolutely too disruptive to the morale of the rest of your staff, or the employee's work is so bad, a severance may be advisable.

Always consider your employees as valuable assets to the company. An unhappy employee is an unproductive employee. It is more costly and time-consuming to train and replace employees than it is to attempt a salvage program, as long as the situation does not reach a point of no return.

When You're the Boss—and You Have Marital Problems

Everyone expects the boss to handle a divorce more effectively and more subtly than his or her subordinates. I agree. I have interviewed hundreds of applicants, before and after divorce. Many of our applicants are managers and CFOs who will honestly relate their feelings to a trusted employment consultant with whom they have developed a good rapport. Never volunteer to advise subordinate accountants on their marital problems—they need a qualified professional. Instead, try to understand the situation and determine whether an applicant who is in the middle of a divorce is suitable for a job interview. Often the aftereffects of a messy, dragged-out divorce result in job loss as well.

☐ A JOB: ALSO A FACT OF LIFE

A Lifetime on the Job

Accountants, like everyone else, will probably work 40 to 50 years of their lives. Most of us never consciously think of our future from a numerical point of view. Early in our careers, we dream that we will always find a wonderful job, make a lot of money, and retire early. But not all our dreams come true. We can, however, consider our careers as fulfilling encounters, by making a series of attitude adjustments.

A lifetime of toil awaits us, so we might as well get used to it. Why not plan to enjoy it—it *is* possible.

The Ideal Job, Elusive as Quicksilver

I got my first full-time job because I got off at the wrong bus stop in Detroit. In 1951 few recent college graduates could afford to own a car. That was a recession year, when jobs were scarce for new professionals. The job I got, inventory control, wasn't the king of job accounting graduates dream about. But I made the best of a barely acceptable situation, and built on it with each passing year.

Try to maintain a positive mental attitude about your next job. You should think of your present job as temporary, since you hope to get promoted someday. If you're president or general manager, you hope the company will become more prosperous. You must think this way despite the fact that you may not be promoted for some time. Not having an objective or a dream is like being in prison. You may never attain the ideal job, but you should never stop trying or visualizing it—because once the spirit of the hunt is gone, that's the end of a potentially fruitful career.

Recessions, Prosperity, and Your Career

Economic recessions are a fact of life. You will probably experience at least five recessions during your career, and you will not be fond of them, since the thought of job loss will loom large on the horizon. You will also experience prosperous times when jobs are plentiful, and your confidence and sense of security are high. At such times, should you be unhappy with your job, the temptation to test the job opportunity waters will be great.

Jobs in the Year 2000

Many of us take our jobs for granted, once we have one that pays reasonably well and has opportunities for promotion. But times are changing. Mergers and reorganizations are making annual promotions obsolete. By the 1990s the competition for the better accounting jobs will get tougher with each passing year. Most new jobs will be created in the restaurant, retail, wholesale, health care, and banking fields. By the year 2000, over 50 percent of the population will be over 35 years old, meaning a more mature competitive base for the ambitious. Not only will there be more competition for your present job, but there will be more competition for the jobs you will be seeking when you decide to make a job change. On the average, accountants will change jobs at least five times throughout their career. Like an athlete, you will be competing throughout your entire career— you might as well settle back and begin pacing yourself for a lifetime of competitiveness.

The Vanishing Breed

The young "hotshot" is a vanishing breed. Self-made men like Lynn Townsend, Bill Agee, and Robert ("Whiz Kid") McNamara, are becoming few and far between. Lynn Townsend was the youngest partner (under 30) at Touche Ross CPAs (Detroit). He eventually became president and chairman at his client company, Chrysler Corporation. William Agee became president of Bendix when he was under 40. Ford Motor Company plucked Robert McNamara right out of the military service, after World War II, along with several other "whiz kids." To get to the top in the future will be a much slower and more difficult process—the cards will be stacked against an ambitious, goal-oriented accountant.

A. Demographics
1. Decreasing birth rates
2. Increasing life span, creating an older talent pool.
3. Executives working longer—to age 70
B. Increasing number of business MBA graduates
C. Complexity of running multinational corporations
D. Slowdown in economic growth—not as many openings

E. The new generation is more affluent, and better educated—
   they've developed new values. (They want high-priced living, but not much self-denial.)

F. Loyalty to company—only if employees' interests are considered first. More loyalty to family and self

G. Mergers and acquisitions, reducing the number of top jobs
   available

3

MASTERING THE ART OF COMPETING

A small percentage of accountants excel consistently. They seem to possess superior abilities when faced with obstacles. How did they get that way?

These super accountants, in early childhood, began a life of inescapable and unending competitiveness. Within their family circle, they were engaged in sibling rivalry to gain parental acceptance, love, or praise. If they were firstborn children, they were likely to be overachievers and highly competitive.

In elementary school, they unconsciously sought recognition by volunteering to do chores that might please their teacher. They did not quite understand that they were beginning to develop their competitive skills. It may not have been until they actually won recognition for superior individual accomplishments (in spelling bees, art projects, and similar activities) that they really understood that they could tap their inner resources when needed. Then they began to comprehend that they had to try even harder and become more efficient to reach their desired goals.

In high school and college, they began to realize how important grades and social behavior were to the development of self-esteem. They could tell who the winners were likely to be, because their victories were predicted in the school yearbook's class prophecy. Could the soothsayers of bygone days have been that accurate?

As professional accountants, you are seeking to attain and maintain successful careers in a field that is increasingly competitive in an uncertain business climate. You know that mastering the art of competition is an absolute must for self-preservation. Accountants are in for the shock of their lives if they join an organization run on traditional principles—the survival of the fittest.

You may have struggled through your college academics and concluded that once you got your diploma, a secure future would be assured. You may have never dreamed that the business world would demand more competitive knowhow than you were able to deliver. You may never have taken the time to develop your competitive skills. What now?

It's a tough business world out there. You had better take it seriously now, and get ready for some tough competitors in the late 1980s and 1990s, because it will not get easier.

You may be wondering if it's too late. Are you too old? Has the die been cast? Not by a long shot. True, you may have some catching up to do; you may be a late bloomer. But competitive skills can be developed at any age and any stage of your career. How well you do will depend entirely on your desire and determination, with a dash of luck. Following are some tips to help you develop those special skills that will make you more competitive.

☐ MATCH YOUR STYLE WITH COMPANY CULTURE

The role you play in your office "family" will determine your eventual success as a competitive executive. Your actions and mannerisms must be in sync with the corporate culture. Learn to understand your company's values, then get into the company spirit. Some companies try to spell out their values in policy manuals, but they seldom succeed in explaining these intricate intangibles.

On a plane from Florida to Detroit about a year ago, I sat next to a young, outgoing computer company executive, who was eager to make conversation. He had just spent a full week of intensive meetings at a West Palm Beach hotel discussing, among other subjects, his company's corporate culture. The merger of his corporation with another was a marriage of two distinct cultures. His company, as a new entity, needed to develop a new, hybrid culture that would fit with both company headquarters—Detroit and New York. Many companies give culture adaptability a high priority when they consider hiring new executives.

Vague terms like *casual, cooperative, sophisticated,* or *laid back* can describe a culture generally. A dress code is sometimes a visual clue to a corporate culture (e.g., not wearing ties, or wearing summer straw fedoras, as employees did at Big Eight CPA firms some years ago).

At a large transportation corporation where I worked for nine years there seemed to be separate subcultures at division headquarters and at corporate headquarters, where I spent my last four years as a senior financial analyst. Although I spent a great deal of time reviewing, and in some cases developing, company manuals, I could not remember anything in writing about these distinct cultures. But I definitely felt the differences. The division staff had a no-nonsense, profit-oriented, keep-busy culture, wherein everyone worked hard and consistently. We always had deadlines and plenty of pressures to go with them. Many accounting sections worked a great deal of overtime. Meanwhile, at corporate headquarters, there was a feeling of serenity. The pace was considerably slower and more tranquil than at division headquarters.

When you change jobs and companies, look for this underlying culture. Ask the personnel department or the hiring executive what is expected of you in this regard.

☐ YOU CAN'T COMPETE WITH A CORONARY

Have you ever visited the coronary care unit of a hospital? If not, and if you have a tremendous desire to reach the top in the accounting or financial field, then you had better visit such a unit soon. It is a vast maze of electronic equipment, monitors, intravenous tubes, and an ever-present medicinal odor. It is depressing to see so many young people there who seem helpless, listless, dependent on doctors, nurses, and machines to take care of them. The vast majority are male, although there are a few females. Each patient has an ashen complexion and a faraway look. It's hard to believe that, several weeks earlier, these were dynamic executives, driving their departments or companies to unattained victory. Periodic health checkups could have kept most of these patients out of the emergency room. When you see these patients, realize that this could be *you,* if you allow your competitive spirit to get completely out of control.

Many accountants see *other* accountants as likely to have heart attacks or job burnout—but not themselves. They notice the clenched jaw and fists of their bosses or subordinates. They seem to think they can tell a "cardiac-prone" employee—an overweight, hypertensive, Type A smoker—when they see one. Not so! I remember when, as a financial analyst with a large corporation, I met my boss for the first time. He was one of the many bosses I had with this firm, which believed in rotating its managers. This executive had been transferred from the South African subsidiary, where he was the CFO. He appeared healthy as an ox to me, but I was wrong. He had recently had a heart attack and had been transferred to the more relaxed, less high-pressure atmosphere of the corporate finance staff. Before the passage of equal employment opportunity legislation, many large companies would fire an employee who had had a heart attack because they felt such employees contributed to high rates of absenteeism and costly disability claims.

In 15 years, hundreds of my job applicants freely have admitted to having suffered heart attacks, some mild, some severe. In only a few of them could I detect that something had happened to them, because their eyes had a faraway, dazed, worn-out look.

Cardiac counseling centers hope to educate and perhaps alleviate the pressure on "high-stressed" individuals. These centers offer a variety of stress management programs to small companies and businesses that are concerned with "cardiac-prone" behavior in employees. These centers aim to target detrimental habits such as smoking, poor diet, and erratic sleeping patterns that lead to serious illness, and to prevent the initial occurrence and recurrence of coronary heart disease.

Cardiac-prone accountants are likely to burn out earlier than their colleagues and, meanwhile, to wreak havoc in the work environment. In the long run, when your department or company keeps stress-related situations to a minimum, the result is a more cost-efficient and productive operation.

Obviously, the best way to recognize your proneness to heart problems is through periodic health checkups. If you have had severe physical problems, are over 50, have high-pressure responsibilities, then semiannual health checkups are recommended. Many doctors work on Saturdays, and your medical bill may be picked up by your health care provider. Even if you do pay out of your own pocket, these checkups are good long-range health investments.

□ EXPECT SOME STRESS—IT CAN HELP YOU COMPETE

A Minneapolis investor in his mid-forties, "Ed Jergens" believes in facing facts: He relishes the tooth-grinding, blood-pumping state of stressful bliss. He says he thrives on it as a way of life. He adds, however, that he probably creates more stress for others than for himself. How true! Another buzzword getting increasing attention in accounting circles is *job stress*. That ominous-sounding phrase is often overused but sometimes underused.

Stress is two-faced. Many accountants think stressful situations are exclusively negative events (a death in the family, losing one's job, divorce, etc.). When a person is threatened, the part of the brain that controls emotions signals the adrenal glands to prepare to fight or run. We usually cannot control this. But stress can occur during positive situations, too—being promoted, getting a raise, getting married, getting a new job. When stress is positive, we can call it a *challenge*. Each person faces roughly 50 to 60 stresses, positive and negative, each day.

A senior accountant being promoted to supervisor may question whether she is worthy of the new challenge, but if she uses all her abilities to advantage, the stress could turn into feelings of satisfaction. This positive stress is known as *eustress*. It is not threatening or uncomfortable. Remember that if nothing ever challenges or stresses you, your job and your life will become very dull.

A certain amount of job stress is absolutely necessary in order for your adrenalin to keep flowing. Stress makes you go forward. But it must be monitored regularly and carefully, or it can get out of hand. Few, if any, accounting jobs have little or no stress, what with month-end and year-end closings, IRS and CPA audits, constant deadlines, and people looking over your shoulder.

As a cost analyst in the early 1950s, I noticed that, in the plant's accounts payable department, a great number of clerical workers (who had month-end deadlines) had experienced heart attacks or job burnouts. Our division financial department which was composed mostly of accountants in their mid-twenties, had considerably fewer.

How much stress do management accountants experience today? Doctors Thomas Holmes and Richard Rahe, both psychiatrists at the University of Washington Medical School, worked out a stress scale of life events. They interviewed hundreds of men and women of different ages, backgrounds, and economic and social classes, asking about the adjustment to these events. Then they ranked the events according to the amount of stress each involved.

Which of these is happening in your life now? Which is yet another urgent reason to do something about your blood pressure? (See Table 3.1.)

My NAA *Management Accounting* magazine, dated March 1982, gave me some insight. J. Patrick Kelly, PhD, professor of business management at Brigham Young University, and Robert H. Strawser, professor of accounting with an MBA from the University of Maryland, conducted a study of job stress involving 138 management accountants from a random sample of accoun-

TABLE 3.1. The Scale of Life Events

Event	Level of Stress
Death of spouse	100
Divorce	73
Marital separation	65
Death of close family member	63
Personal injury or illness	53
Marriage	50
Fired at work	47
Marital reconciliation	45
Retirement	45
Change in health of family member	44
Pregnancy	40
Business readjustment	39
Change in financial state	38
Death of close friend	37
Change to different line of work	36
Change in number of arguments with spouse	35
Mortgage over $10,000	31
Foreclosure of mortgage or loan	30
Change in responsibilities at work	29
Son or daughter leaving home	29
Outstanding personal achievement	28
Wife begins or stops work	26
Change in living conditions	25
Revision of personal habits	24
Trouble with boss	23
Change in work hours or conditions	20
Change in residence	20
Change in recreation	19
Change in social activities	18
Vacation	13
Christmas	12

tants working in industry, drawn from the membership of AICPA. The survey queried the respondent on a number of personal and job-related variables to determine whether any were significantly related to job stress. The variables were:

1. Age
2. Educational level
3. Annual income
4. Sex
5. Marital status

6. Number of children
7. Title of position
8. Management level
9. Number of subordinates
10. Number of years experience in accounting
11. Number of years experience in current position
12. Number of others reporting to same superior
13. Percentage of time spent on travel
14. Number of hours worked last week

Surprisingly, only two of the 14 factors were associated with high levels of job stress:

1. *Age:* Older management accountants tended to report higher levels of job stress than did their younger colleagues.
2. *Management level:* More job stress was found for individuals holding higher level positions than for those in lower level positions.

My observations over the past 15 years are generally in agreement with these findings. It makes sense that older accountants' physical and mental resources have been more taxed by stressful situations than have those of younger accountants. There are always exceptions, like the case of the accountant whose boss truly dislikes his subordinate and intentionally makes life difficult for him. Then, stress can be unbearable, and some critical decisions must be made or a serious health problem can result. I would suggest a discussion with the boss to bring out these unjustified tirades. If no common ground is reached, perhaps it is time to ask for a transfer or look for another job. It also makes sense that executive accountants, with the preponderance of responsibilities lying on their shoulders, can and do get involved in more meaningful and stressful decision-making situations, the results of which can lose money for the company, lose jobs for thousands of people, or even ruin the company. Decisions at the top can cause more destruction or greater accomplishments than decisions at the middle or lower management level.

Daily Goal-Setting Success Can Help Reduce Stress

If you don't know where you are going, any road map will direct you there. To avoid stress, you must set reasonably attainable goals. Completing most of your small goals during one work day will work wonders for your confidence and self-esteem. Obviously, you want to complete the entire assignment or at least your immediate objectives. I recall planning the details of an important assignment I had as a cost analyst at a division of an auto firm. I had a one-week deadline to submit, in writing, "A Proposal to Eliminate the Drain Plug (gas tank)"—a proposal I had initiated after a cost analysis of material cost variances. After the week's deadline, it was to be submitted to the division product planning committee.

I broke up the week into five work days, with specific tasks for each day. On 3 × 5 cards I wrote up each day's goal, and I carried the cards in my pocket for quick review. Although I had five specific goals, I began requesting all statistical information on the first day to allow for unavoidable delays.

First day: Call, at random, 10 auto dealers' service departments re service calls for emptying gas tank by unscrewing drain plug.

Second day: Find out how many drain plugs were produced annually by corporation. This would be the volume used for a profit analysis.

Third day: Develop material, labor, and burden cost of plug.

Fourth day: Analyze and work out dollar cost savings to corporation if plug eliminated, and write up study.

Fifth day: Review and discuss results with boss. If favorable, have report typed, ready to present to committee.

The preceding analysis did not take eight hours each day. Other (non–drain plug) assignments and routine tasks were performed while I waited for specific assignment information.

I'm happy to say I met the deadline: The proposal was submitted to the committee. Initially turned down (for political reasons, I later found out), two years later the proposal was approved and saved the company millions of dollars. Ironically, both my boss and I had been promoted and transferred to other company locations by that time.

Since habits control 90 percent of what you do, to avoid stress you must adjust and redirect your habits and energy toward your priorities and needs.

Do Most Important Work When You Are Sharpest

If at all possible, schedule your most important or most high-pressure work at your most productive time. If you don't know when that is, find out quickly! I have used this technique for years. It works for me. I am most efficient and energetic roughly from 8:00 A.M. to noon. Therefore, I attempt to schedule important meetings, interviews, phone conversations, and difficult decisions for my most productive period. It doesn't always turn out as planned, of course. Many times certain work, interviews, or meetings need to be rescheduled for other times.

Cultivate Rest and Relaxation Habits

Get sufficient rest and relaxation—your competition does. Unless you want to become a workaholic, you must learn to earn your leisure time. You can judge workaholics by the hours they work. Workaholics have an addiction to work that is compulsive and irrational. For the workaholic, the idea of a vacation is a contradiction in terms. To avoid this addiction, pick activities that will keep your mind off your job—family outings, movies, dinners, golf, evenings out with friends. Take a laugh break or a mood-altering break. Seek out a co-worker who will make you laugh. At home, put on a funny TV program. Play with your children or your dog or cat.

Body Maintenance

Develop regular exercise techniques, stop smoking, and culti- vate a proper diet. These routines could do wonders in alleviating the effects of stress situations. There is no excuse for nonhereditary obesity or a run-down appearance in the office. It does not help your self-image in face-to-face discussions or confrontations with your superiors.

Since you put in 58 percent of your week working, you should prepare yourself mentally and physically for each new workday. Professional athletes do, so why not you as a professional accountant? Take regular vacations; you'll keep your competitive edge. With a well-rested mind, you'll come up with better ideas and do sharper work than those who always have their noses to the grindstone.

Emotional Outlets

You need someone to whom to tell your work troubles. If you don't have anyone now, it's not too late to seek out someone close to you (a co-worker, relative, friend, or neighbor). It should be someone who likes you, is a sincere and sympathetic listener, and understands you—someone who can be objective and somewhat critical at the same time. Be careful not to relegate this person to a role of a father confessor. At times, things will get very rough for you, and you'll need to let off steam—preferably outside the office.

Procrastination

The derivation of the word *procrastinate* tells its own story. It comes from the Latin *pro* ("forward')' and *cras* ("tomorrow"). Most accountants admit to some procrastination in their daily work routines. The degree of procrastination you exercise on important matters can cause you severe stress, especially if you miss deadlines.

Your work habits must be adjusted so that you begin your assignments in enough time to meet deadlines. If your superiors do not give you enough time, I suggest you take work home. This will not add to your personal comfort, but it will help alleviate stress because you will get the assignment done on time.

Overreaction to Stress

Suppose your car gets a flat tire, and you're late for work. The bank calls to say you're $50 overdrawn on your checking account. It's that kind of Monday, and you can feel the knots in your stomach as you reach for another cigarette or another cup of coffee. These daily pressures could be killing you without your knowing it. Overreacting to such stress can make you a prime candidate for illness or sudden death, according to Dr. Robert S. Eliot, the man one medical journal calls the "high priest of stress management" (Eliot, 1982, p. 8A). At age 44, Eliot suffered his own heart attack—ironically, in the middle of a lecture on how to prevent heart attacks. He has since made a complete recovery, but the trauma made him rethink his life. Eliot is now a consultant to various government and top business firms, as well as chairman of the Department of Preventive and Stress Medicine at the University of Nebraska Medical Center.

Take being a CFO for a steel firm, one of the hottest jobs in the United States. On the outside, the CFO may appear cool and unruffled, handling one problem after another. But inside, the stress may be causing his body to go bananas. His heart is working as hard as if he were running up three flights of stairs. His blood pressure is up. The resistance against his pumping heart has tripled. According to Dr. Eliot, it's like driving 55 miles per hour with the brakes on.

Awareness of stress is one way to protect yourself. If you are a hot "reactor," you may recognize that you can be productive without being destructive. If you have concluded that your job is stressful, and that stress is downright dangerous, you must ask yourself whether it is important enough to be worth dying for. It all boils down to your attitude toward your job, your career objectives, and above all your ideas on self-preservation.

Make the Most of Deadline Pressure

If you have a deadline to meet, use pressure for your benefit. When you're under the gun, concentration is your best friend, a wandering mind your opponent. Here are a few workable suggestions to help you stay focused:

1. Make a sign that briefly names the assignment, with the due date in large letters. Tape it on the wall in your home, office, and car.

2. Postpone or cancel unimportant assignments or activities.

3. Originate your own penalty for *not* finishing the project on time—say, not going to the football or hockey game if you miss.

4. Tell your associates about your deadline, and offer to buy all of them coffee or a drink if you don't make it.

5. Close your office door at home or at work. If there are too many distractions at your desk, work in an empty meeting room.

☐ WHAT YOU CAN DO TO MINIMIZE STRESS IN YOUR SUBORDINATES

1. Delegating assignments allows subordinates enough authority to carry out the responsibilities assigned. A letter or a phone call to other departments involved in the assignment, announcing your employees' responsibilities, will help them get cooperation from their peers and from the supervisory people involved.

2. Be clear about the scope and responsibilities of the assignment. In a face-to-face meeting, give information slowly, using simple language, and then ask if the directions are understood. Ask directly if employees think they can complete the assignment on time. Ask if they foresee any problems. The average person remembers only 9 percent of what he reads and 18 percent of what he hears. From a practical standpoint, it is probably better to discuss an assignment in person than to write it out.

3. Routinely follow up progress. Keep your door open to subordinates in case they run into unexpected problems but hesitate to ask questions for fear they may lose ground with you.

4. Let your subordinates know they were chosen because they were qualified. Tell them they were the right ones for the assignment.

5. Give a specific calendar deadline for completion of the project. Be flexible enough that an extension can be granted if problems arise. If deadlines are firm, let your subordinates know.

6. Make sure the people who work for you don't have the wrong jobs. They may be in over their heads, or overqualified, or even bored stiff with the job. You may not be absolutely sure about these problems; judgment and personnel input will have to prevail.

7. There could be a great deal of difference between what subordinates perceive their jobs to be and what supervisors really expect. Try to reduce the "great deal" to a minimum of difference.

8. Institute new programs on coping with the job. Relaxation techniques, listening, hobbies, weight control, or stress management training sessions should be encouraged. Companies like John Hancock Mutual Life, Texas Instruments, and Pepsico already have such programs.

☐ IF STRESS ALREADY IS YOUR PROBLEM, REVERSE IT

What if stress has you in its grip and you feel as though you are drowning? You have so much difficulty coping that you are considering resigning. Perhaps you are even on the verge of being fired.

1. If your aggressive personality is resulting in tension-filled days on the job, back off. Evaluate: Not every argument is worth trying to win. Defend values that are important (for example, ethics), but learn to ignore lesser issues (such as desk seating arrangements).

2. Look for causes. Analyze the actions or words that caused your stress in the first place. Visualize a better way to react that won't cause you such grief, and be determined to use it if the same stressful situation happens again.

3. When stress builds up at the office, step up your home leisure activity. Take time after work to do something you like—indulge in outdoor activities (tennis, golf, gardening), go to a

movie, read a book or magazine, go to a restaurant, or relax by running or jogging.

4. Dismiss petty remarks. Don't worry over things your boss said to you. As long as the remark was not job-threatening, let it go.

5. Don't feel you must physically stay in a stressful office. Go for a walk, or get a cup of coffee, as far away from your work station as possible.

6. Change your life-style or work habits. A doctor's assistance may help you avoid more serious sickness. Consider biofeedback, exercise, or meditation. Seek help from your church leader or a psychologist or social worker who is trained to suggest various stress reduction techniques.

Pay more attention to your feelings and jot down periods when stress occurs. Try to determine who and what are the stressors in your life. Don't be too surprised if it's not the boss who is causing you these problems. The boss may only be the scapegoat. Look at home for stress stemming from family situations. Be objective and, above all, be honest with yourself.

7. Kick the caffeine and sugar habits. Find substitutes. The more evidence I collect about these two, the more I agree with physicians and psychiatrists who say that they do a lot of harm. I kicked the cigarette habit years ago. Now I'm working on sugar.

8. Body aches are messages to you. Remember that stress is your body's way of reacting to high-pressure situations. However, you are in control of your thoughts; your thoughts cannot control you unless you allow them to. Take charge of your life, and practice stress management. Tension, fear, and self-doubt can block peak performance. These reactions are all passing on messages to you. Listen.

☐ LIVE POSITIVE THINKING

We are bombarded today by religious TV programs and business seminars on positive thinking as applied to everyday living and business life. Books and tapes by such noted authors as Dale Carnegie, Norman Vincent Peale, and Dr. Robert H. Schuller are available to encourage you. I feel very strongly about the

power of positive thinking. I believe that all accountants fall
into certain categories when it comes to how positive or how
negative their thinking is. Which are you?

Positive always?

Positive most of the time?

Positive some of the time?

Negative most of the time?

Negative always?

It's important to think positively on the job because it's almost
impossible to steer a job into a successful career path without
first believing that you can do it.

Most personnel executives prefer candidates who exhibit
positive attitudes in the job interview. Most hiring executives,
assuming the right chemistry and technical knowhow are
present, hire candidates who have a positive nature and can
make the hiring executive feel good about hiring this person.

How Positive Should You Be?

There is a limit, of course. I can still remember the time I was
being interviewed for what I thought was the corporate controller position of a small auto supplier in the Detroit area. The
president, CFO, and chief engineer sat at a round table during
the interview, and we all had tea and cookies. It was 10:00 A.M.,
my best time of day, and I had prepared positively the night
before and had had a good night's sleep and fine breakfast. I was
very confident about myself and my credentials.

Mentally, I was ready; I felt positive about myself. In fact, the
interview went off so well that I sounded absolutely too good to
be true. I passed around my article, recently published by the
NAA Bulletin, on "Cost Accounting and the Engineering Department." It was a smash-hit interview—but I did not get the
job. The reason—a communication gap. The three executives
were interviewing me for the CFO position, which was open, at
a salary twice that of the controller position—which was *not*
open. When the triumvirate asked me about the salary I was

earning, they almost fell over backwards, since I was earning only half the salary they had in mind for the CFO position. They did not make the offer because my interview was better than my qualifications. (Two years later, this same company did have the corporate controller position open, and I was called again by the president. By that time, however, I had changed careers and had committed myself to the recruiting field, so I could not pursue the offer.) The lesson: Positive thinking can do wonders, but it's not enough—we also must be technically qualified.

Positive Habits Can Be Developed

You are not born with positive habits; you must develop them. Throughout your career, will have ups and downs, from positive always all the way down to negative always and back up again. This doesn't mean that, if you are successful, you will always think positively. But if you think positively (and live out your positive thoughts), you are more likely to be successful, assuming you have also prepared yourself technically. Your degree of success will depend on how good you really are, as well as on some luck, your skill at office politics, perseverance, and other variables.

In thinking positively, you will attract positive activity and create your own reality. You can fulfill your career goals by having complete faith in your own mind and overcoming subconscious destructive thoughts that prevent you from attaining your objectives. Even people who are mildly depressed, vaguely disenchanted, underachievers, or downright mediocre can improve their business lives by acquiring positive thinking as a way of life. It's a risk worth taking.

Dale Carnegie, the tirelessly optimistic Missouri farm boy, began winning friends and influencing people as far back as 1936, over 50 years ago. There's little that's new or unique in this philosophy. Nowadays, though, you have to do even better to be a success. How can you improve your self-confidence and self-esteem? How can you unlock your full potential and achieve your heart's desire?

Career success is a do-it-yourself project. No one else can do it for you. The only thing that can keep you from overproducing is yourself. You must learn to know yourself better and create a genuine personal transformation. Change is an absolute in business. Managing change is the only way to achieve superior performance—and superior performance is the only way to survive.

All the positive thinking in the world will get you nowhere in your accounting career unless you start with a serious intention and develop a reasonable goal. Don't wait for divine inspiration. By setting a goal, you take responsibility for your own career. If you don't like where you are in that career, it's nobody's fault but your own. You have the power to make changes by tapping your inner resources. But first you must feel good about yourself. This feeling helps you develop energy.

Don't use your past as a crutch. Negative thoughts—anger, resentment, prejudice—are just alibis for not taking charge of yourself. Blaming something or someone else for your shortcomings is simply not valid. Don't let negative thoughts overwhelm you psychologically. Don't be a prisoner of such thoughts— dispense with them.

Many successful accounting executives know that, if you put minimum effort and concentration into your job, you cannot expect to get maximum fulfillment.

☐ LEARN TO COPE WITH YOUR BOSS

I've had plenty of experience in handling bosses. In my 16-year accounting career, with five different companies, I progressed from junior accountant to corporate controller of a multiplant corporation. I can still remember each of the different bosses that I reported to directly. My bosses had different temperaments, personalities, and drives. In one stretch with a large corporation, I had ten different bosses in nine years. This resulted from a combination of my own promotions and bosses' transfers or changes in status, as well as centralization and decentralization at different divisions, groups, and corporate headquarters.

I learned early in my career that my relationship with my boss was based on mutual dependence and understanding. Bosses seldom make major changes to adjust to their subordinates, but they do make minor adjustments and become aware of subordinates' personal attitudes and needs. But as soon as I had developed a good rapport with one boss, along came a new one. In self-defense, I learned the art of managing my boss. I can remember one manager who was very likable and generous. He believed in a lot of socializing after work with his employees and their families. Another cost analysis manager liked to go out with the boys after softball games, to local bars and night spots. He had excellent management skills, and his staff went all out for him. The next boss was a great technician, not strong on personality, but a hard driver and a good motivator. We were so highly motivated that we were all eager to work through part of our lunch hour, to find out ways to save costs in the adjacent plant. From the company's standpoint, this boss was most productive and profit-oriented. My next manager delegated everything and often left me alone without assignments or supervision. When I approached him about the apparent lack of work, he replied, "You're here to think, not to work. Just be ready when the assignments come." Good assignments eventually did come, but since building departmental empires was in vogue at the company, and I felt I got lost in the shuffle, during this period I began looking for another job. My next boss was completely overqualified for his managerial position; he had been division controller of one of his company's overseas operations. He was recuperating from a heart attack, developed almost no rapport, and delegated everything to his qualified subordinates, who sank or swam with each assignment.

And so the boss game went on. Each new manager was a pleasant change, a challenge, and a game for me.

How to Handle Your New Boss: Some Tips

1. Don't try to impress the boss at first. A good boss will see through this façade. Be yourself, friendly but businesslike. Wait for signals from the boss to move to a closer level of rapport—or to a more distant level. It's imperative that you study your boss's work style.

2. Run, don't walk. Even a simple assignment should be performed in high gear. I prided myself on being the best

"go-fer" in the 30-person product analysis department. I didn't walk—I ran (in reality, I walked fast). I was a fantastic runner. I did not feel my role as a go-fer was dehumanizing since I also did a creditable job on my analytical assignments. Do your job well and with zest, no matter what the assignment is—your efforts will be noticed and acknowledged.

3. My neighbor, Daniel J. Picklo, a Harvard MBA graduate with 10 years financial analysis experience with General Motors Corporation, told me he believes in helping to promote his boss. He thinks it's a good idea to make the boss look good. His advice: Study your new boss's habits—his goals, pressures, ethics, strengths, and weaknesses. I would add: Take time to note what pleases and displeases the boss, not what pleases and displeases you. Your job is to satisfy the boss's business objectives and needs. For example, does he prefer receiving information in written form or verbally? A compatible relationship with your boss is essential to being efficient on your job. Picture the boss as the person who represents the company. You can always rationalize that you will be helping the company by pleasing the boss, even if you don't exactly see eye to eye with him. Developing a positive attitude toward your boss will make life easier for you from 9:00 to 5:00. Remember, the boss is only 50 percent of your relationship with him. You are not going to alter your basic personality, nor will he. But you should be aware of any serious differences and work around them.

4. Don't take slights and oversights personally. We all expect our bosses to be perfect, but they have shortcomings just as we do. If the boss forgets to smile or say hello, or even fails to acknowledge you, don't take offense. Many bosses have a broader scope of responsibilities than we have; they have more serious things to think about, and know how to concentrate on the task at hand. Quickly discover the boss's moods. Listen attentively. Your boss may be worried or concentrating on impending or real problems that you may not be aware of. Its all right for *you* to say hello first.

5. Don't overinfluence the boss. It's all right to influence the boss's decisions, but don't overdo it. A capable manager will appreciate input from subordinates and will even accept occa-

sional judicious criticism. But once a decision is made, even over your aggressive objections, drop your criticism and go along with the decision, even if you're sure it was wrong. If the boss has made the wrong decision—one that you did not agree with—he'll pay more attention to your ideas next time.

6. Never downgrade or slander your boss, even if it is justified. This is the fastest way to the guillotine. Word will eventually get around that you are not a loyal employee, and that is a death sentence.

7. Allow your boss to get most, if not all, of the credit. As a subordinate, you may feel your boss is getting all the credit, unfairly, for work you have done. But remember, your boss may have guided you on these projects, perhaps even trained you. Let the boss take the credit—you will get your chance. Help your boss get promoted so you can be recommended for his job. This shows business maturity and trust in your relationship with the boss.

8. Develop superior work habits. As Lee Iacocca said, "There are no free lunches. In the end, you've got to be productive" (Iacocca, 1984). There is a certain amount of discipline you must maintain in order to administer your function. If your job is nine-to-five, be there before 9:00—eager to get started. Stay longer if you must to complete assignments on a timely basis. Continual lateness for work shows a disregard for rules and expresses too much independence, which may not blend into the corporate culture. Always give the respect that's due the position, even if you do not respect the person in that position.

9. Blowing your top at the boss is bad, but it's not the end—unless it happens over and over again. If you yelled at the boss because your 10-page report was criticized, don't despair. I doubt that there's a boss alive today who has not been told off by a subordinate at least once. Make sure your boss is not humiliated, though. A disciplined boss usually won't yell back at you, but will remember the incident for a long, long time.

The best thing for the subordinate to do is to offer an honest apology at the next opportune moment. A simple explanation of your anger will suffice. Then bury the incident. Even if you think you were justified, never try to excuse your behavior.

You will have learned a useful lesson—not to get that upset again over things that are beyond your control.

10. Always look your boss squarely in the eye. Speak in a firm but pleasant voice. Many managers perceive good eye contact as evidence of confidence and concentration on what they are saying.

11. Learn all you can about your job. This will give you a competitive edge. Henry Ford, for example, watched men working on cars at his factory and noticed they spent a lot of time walking back and forth between the cars. Instead of the man going to the car, Ford reasoned, the car should go to the man. Out of that unusual idea came the assembly line.

12. Don't waste the boss's time. Be concise, and don't force conversation with the boss when you really have nothing to say. Such efforts will appear to be a weakness, a transparent attempt to impress the boss. Unless you are absolutely sure your boss is receptive, don't volunteer any discussion of your home or marital problems. Many bosses will discuss business or career problems, but nothing personal. Time is a manager's most important resource, so be as brief as you can in giving your boss routine information. Let the boss ask you for more detail.

☐ LEARN TO COPE WITH A YOUNGER BOSS

1. A younger boss who is qualified is not a great problem. If your boss is truly competent but is much younger than you, you should have only a minor adjustment problem. You should not view the boss's youthfulness as a major obstacle to your progress on the job, just a minor problem you can solve by adjusting your attitude.

There is no business rule that says older employees should not be supervised by younger ones, or that age implies competence. You must assume your boss deserves this status and responsibility, and also deserves your cooperation. This is not the place for petty jealousy to rear its ugly head.

My boss at a giant corporation once brought in a new financial analysis supervisor from outside the company. He was younger than most of us on the staff who had thought that we were competing for that supervisory job. But my initial jealousy and hurt didn't last long, because this young man anticipated our feelings and, through his actions, proved to us that he deserved the job. Eventually, we even got to like him. He made sure of that.

2. Help train a younger boss. If your boss lacks experience and maturity, and has been placed in this position to gain experience because of his untapped talent and potential, so be it. You can still enjoy your job and help the company by training a new executive. It's a good opportunity for you to show your talents as a developer of executives.

The decision to hire this younger supervisor has already been made—you can't do anything about it. So make up your mind to be a good team player. It will do wonders for your well-being, not to mention your survival.

Your boss is probably sharp enough to anticipate some problems from older subordinates. Should you decide to be his enemy, he will be ready for you. A fight with a younger boss can only be a no-win situation for you.

Expect your boss to have lots of energy, and try to begin the day as energized as your boss. Pick up his work style to show him you are definitely on his side. Don't give him any opportunity to think that you will not make the grade because of sour grapes brought on by a generation gap.

☐ LEARN TO COPE WITH AN OLDER BOSS

A generation gap calls for some special attention. There is no doubt that working for someone old enough to be your father has some drawbacks. It also has some benefits.

How can you enjoy working with a father figure? If you develop a good father–son relationship, it will be easy. If you do not, however, and if the boss reminds you of your too demanding dad, then you may have a problem. Again, it's up to *you* to adjust your attitude, not the other way around. Tell yourself, "This person has a wealth of experience, and I have a wonderful opportunity to tap his wisdom." My first boss in accounting was an assistant to the vice-president of finance of a large manufacturing firm; he was old enough to be my father, and I looked up to him as an all-wise parent. Once, I almost lost my job when he challenged my ideas and figures. I stuck to my guns, and I happened to be right. From then on, our relationship blossomed. Although he had a reputation as difficult to work for, for me he wasn't. I had the proper attitude for a cantankerous, tough-minded boss who was known for chewing up assistants. I had developed the secret of handling bosses.

☐ WHAT YOUR BOSS EXPECTS OF YOU

Let's discuss some ideas that you may not want to consider. Like all constructive criticism, these ideas will do you some good in your quest for accounting career success. Few of my accounting applicants have ever gone out of their way to think clearly about what makes them tick. Do you really know what your business character is? Have you ever added up your assets and liabilities, and come up with your net worth? Do you know, for example, what you have to accomplish to make yourself valuable to your company? Determine:

Your technical aptitudes

Your personal characteristics

The interests and talents you can develop that will make you more valuable to your employer, and consequently to yourself

The most difficult thing to do is to admit your failings and shortcomings to yourself. You should make every effort to overcome them and, at the very least, face them honestly by adapting your career plans to those you are unable to resolve. Based on your daily job performance, the most important questions you can ask yourself are:
Would you

hire yourself?

promote yourself?

fire yourself?

Besides self-assessment, there is another way to measure the value of what you give to your job—what bosses think their subordinates should do for them to meet their management objectives favorably. A company expects of its employees certain qualities that go beyond technical qualifications. These qualities, which everyone wants to have, regardless of job situation, can be summarized in four general categories:

Courage
Confidence
Enthusiasm
Goal orientation

Courage

Courage is the quality hiring executives always seek but seldom find. It has been accurately stated that fear defeats more people than any other single characteristic. Worry is closely related to fear. The accountant whose mind is troubled by worries cannot do a good job. The best way to stop worrying is to realize that you are afraid of something, and that you can overcome that fear. That takes courage.

There are on-the-job situations that also call for courage. We are all familiar with the "yes man" who fades over the long run because he is afraid—he has no mind of his own. (Or, if he has one, he is ready to abandon it to the highest bidder.) Being a fearless person does not mean fighting every decision. That is foolish and lacks even the advantage of gaining you a temporarily favorable position. I have never met an employer who truly liked a yes man. But I have never met a boss who liked a subordinate who was constantly putting him down.

Why is courage important? Your entire career will consist of a combination of successes and failures. All successful people believe that their failures have helped them to become better performers in their pursuits. For example, suppose you took the CPA exam and failed two parts. By failing two parts, you found out that you may not have studied hard enough, or you're not as good a test-taker as you thought, or you could have learned more about the technical aspects of accounting. Somewhere, you missed. Your early mistakes can be reversed, however, and your failures bring out the need to strengthen certain weak areas and set up a new objective in your competitive life. This takes courage.

Confidence

With courage comes the second attribute, confidence. The ability to make your own decisions and stick by them is rare, and is highly regarded by management. Good decision makers frown on indecision and doubt. I believe every successful individual possesses a natural attitude of self-confidence. You and you alone possess this power, but tapping it and mastering your own destiny can often be difficult. The average accountant is confident during much of the business day, but not 100 percent and probably not every day. Just as your moods change from day to day, so does your confidence level.

Attempt to be confident consistently—day to day, week to week. You must have a determined desire; you should be willing to sacrifice and give up personal pleasures in order to satisfy this desire.

Let's assume you are not satisfied with your degree of confidence at this time. What can you do? Obviously, wishing alone will not do it. You must have a plan to develop or improve your confidence yourself. I have found the following method of maintaining confidence levels consistently:

1. Courses in developing self-confidence are available in community colleges and local adult education classes. To be meaningful, such courses must be taken repeatedly over the years. As with sports, if you don't practice, your skill tends to drift away without your noticing it.

2. You can improve your communication skills by participating in Toastmasters International or Dale Carnegie. These organizations have proved invaluable to me in developing confidence.

3. For over 20 years I have used subconscious, autosuggestion techniques. If used correctly and continuously, they work. Of the many professional cassette tapes available, my favorite is a record by Frank MacCormack, "Self-Confidence," produced by

Stanford Institute. Fortunately, I have a cassette tape player in my car. However, a headset cassette player will do just as well. Five days a week, on the way to work, I alternate between the tape on "Enthusiasm" and the one on "Self-Confidence." The lessons may be boring day after day, but when the subconscious picks up the message, it becomes almost automatic. Another good time to make effective use of the tapes is just before retiring, when again, your subconscious mind takes over and does most of the work.

The self-assurance, voice, bodily posture, handshake, and facial expression you develop in this way will eventually become natural habits.

Enthusiasm

Nothing important was ever achieved without enthusiasm. Enthusiasm is the outward reflection of our internal confidence.

Some accountants radiate energy as they go about their job, no matter how mundane their actual work. Others show enthusiasm only when exciting things occur—for example, their annual budget plan presentation being accepted the first time it was submitted. Still other accountants go about their routine chores as if they truly were chores—and it shows.

If you're one of those accountants who find it very difficult to show enthusiasm while working, you may never have developed the habit. Over the years, you have probably accepted yourself as a low-key individual who functions well otherwise, and you are satisfied—or were, until you read this paragraph. Approximately 90 percent of the clients who hire accountants through our company desire an outwardly enthusiastic person who is also technically qualified. Very seldom do we receive job specifications indicating a need for an unenthusiastic or unemotional candidate. The same is true for junior accountants, managers, controllers, treasurers, and CFOs.

For our consulting staff, we would not dream of hiring an unenthusiastic person. Generating enthusiasm will not ensure success, but it definitely will help if you have everything else going for you as well. Any success you have in your accounting career will be partly due to your maintaining your enthusiasm over the years. How can you do it? Plan a program of education to kill a bad habit and develop a good new habit.

My suggestions to you are as follows:

1. Take Dale Carnegie sales courses regularly. Repeat them when you feel the need.

2. Study books like *Enthusiasm Makes the Difference* by Dr. Norman Vincent Peale (1967).

3. Many cassette tapes on enthusiasm are available. I have used and played "How to Develop the Power of Enthusiasm" by Paul J. Meyer (Success Motivation Institute), over and over again for years while driving my car to work.

4. Public speaking courses and Toastmasters attendance and membership are excellent outlets for practicing and developing enthusiasm.

5. Practice autosuggestion in front of the mirror while getting ready for work. Silently repeat "I will be enthusiastic" for 10 minutes every morning. Don't be concerned that people will wonder about your new attitude. It will not come about all at once; it will develop slowly. If people do notice your new enthusiasm, they'll be pleased. When enthusiasm declines, an employee's job performance begins to suffer. It's difficult to do a good job when you don't feel like it—when you lack enthusiasm.

6. Develop a curiosity about your company. At first, all I knew about my company was what I read in the papers. Study your company's annual report so you'll have a feel for what kind of company you work for. Interest in a job can be developed only by learning all you can about your job and your work assignments. Have you obtained as much education as you need to compete with your peers—or to surpass them?

Tips on Developing Confidence

1. Pick a role model. If you admire Lieutenant Colonel Oliver North's warm, confident way of speaking, try to develop a

similar style. Remember, you will never be exactly like your role model, but you can copy certain character habits you admire most. My early role models were former presidents Franklin D. Roosevelt and John F. Kennedy. Perhaps the president or chairman of your company has certain traits of character you would like to acquire.

2. Try to change your weaknesses one at a time. If you have had trouble remembering people's names, take a memory course. When I was promoted to a job that required a lot of reading, I took a speed-reading course offered by my company.

3. Establish a mental picture of yourself as a confident individual. Keep repeating to yourself in private (in the car, in the bathroom, while getting ready to fall asleep), "I am a confident individual."

4. Pat yourself on the back when you do a good job. Don't worry if no one else gives you credit—you recognize your achievement. That should make you feel better and will help your self-esteem.

5. If you don't feel confident, fake it, at least at first. Act confident. With constant repetition, this habit will become genuine and automatic. This method worked for me during my accounting career, especially when I was interviewing for a new job.

6. Finally, keep a good opinion of yourself. You're only human, and you will make mistakes, but don't magnify your mistakes.

The enthusiasm you develop on the job may carry over into your personal life, making your life more enjoyable and exciting after 5:00 P.M. as well.

Goal Orientation

You control your own career destiny. You can become as good as you set out to be, as long as you have a goal in mind and are determined to attain it. You won't be handed success on a silver platter—you must earn it by hard work.

One positive thing about failure is that it is only temporary. You can usually try again and again. Remember when your dad or mom kept putting you right back on your bike after each spill, until you learned to balance? That was probably one of your early experiences with failure and success. You knew that sooner or later you would learn to ride that bike, and your parents were always there to protect you from serious harm. In business, unfortunately, you don't have anyone around except, perhaps, a good boss who may watch over you while you compete. Since you are on your own, you can determine the extent of temporary failure you are willing to take.

If you are one of those pessimists who, after failing, says, "What's the use, I'll just fail again," then you probably will. If you want to program yourself not to fail, say to yourself, "I know I failed on the project before, but not this time."

Suppose someone else gets the manager's job you wanted. Are you a failure? You aren't, but you could become a failure if you think you are. A cost accounting supervisor position once opened up at one of my company's plants. I really wanted that job, but didn't get it, although I was qualified. My boss remarked that it was better for my career path to be at the division level than to be a plant supervisor. Perhaps, but I was very disappointed. Yet this disappointment strengthened me, made me more mature, and prepared me for the future. Learn to anticipate disappointments and failures and take them with a grain of salt. Continue to be goal-oriented and think positively, even if unfair decisions temporarily derail your career track.

☐ ARE YOU POWER DRIVEN?

Most accountants don't admit they are seeking power. We all talk about our need for achievement, recognition, and so forth, but we seldom tell anyone, even friends or family, that we are, in effect, seeking power.

People who have little power are more prone to depression and other mental problems. In planning your career, you should try to determine just how much power you will need in order to feel successful. When people do attain power, they often become exhilarated.

People in authority find it necessary to put some distance between themselves and their subordinates. This can also lead to isolation at the top, a feeling of loneliness because there are no peers with whom to discuss common problems. Isolated leaders may begin to think they are all-knowing and all-powerful.

If you generally don't like people to disagree with you, it's a sign that you need power. People who make a mistake and then blame others probably have a need for power and control. They are not able to cope with other people's shortcomings or weaknesses. If you enjoy just being yourself, without feeling you need to be in charge, then your need for power is not too great. Americans are proud of having a high need to achieve, but dislike being told they have a high need for power.

Accountants who aggressively seek legitimate power have a good chance for accelerated career advancement. To gain power, with a solid base, requires you to learn minute details about the organization: its culture, systems, procedures, and chain of command. Gaining power requires a knowledge of special alliances and enemies. You need to know who has the real power. When bosses intimidate or manipulate you, they are knowingly using their power on you. How, then, do you go about gaining power?

1. Keep your boss happy—this takes precedence over other departmental activities.

2. If your subordinates make errors, make sure you let them know, but courteously. Don't let them feel put down.

3. Force yourself to be nice to your superiors even if you despise them—it may mean your job.

4. Remember, the smartest or most productive worker doesn't always get promoted, although those characteristics are very important. The boss has to know that you are smart and productive. If you have not shown your strengths, so that there is no doubt how your boss feels about your abilities, it won't matter how sharp or productive you may be. Learn how to market your pluses to your bosses.

5. Managers must show they are in charge. Being firm, yet courteous and considerate, is an indelible mark of an effective superior. This kind of boss can generate loyalty from subordinates and keep wounded feelings to a minimum.

I spent nine years with a large company naively believing that hard work, loyalty, and perseverance alone would earn me a promotion. In that time I don't think I even came close to a significant promotion, although I moved up in job classification and got raises regularly. I never learned how to mingle with my bosses; I didn't even try. I felt there was no need for that: They should know how good I was. They probably did know, but it didn't matter. I was not political, and I didn't care, although I did want to be promoted. No one, not even my company friends, told me that power and politics go together like salt and pepper.

Office politics is the art of maneuvering for a better place in the organization. Accountants who have difficulty mastering the art of politics often try to substitute idealism. The realities of business may be unpleasant to many, but they are a fact of life.

Regardless of your own thoughts about the dynamics of hierarchy, it is very important for you to have a realistic view of how your organization operates in order not to be hurt by power politics. Many unemployed controllers have admitted to me, behind closed doors, that they lost their job because they were not political. They were dismayed when I asked them, "Why not?"

If it's true that you learn from your mistakes, I must have learned one lesson very well, because I made the same mistake over and over again, year after year. I took pride in believing that I wasn't a "brown-noser." I was even prouder of believing I did not play politics—as if *politics* were a dirty word.

If I had to do it over again, I would learn office politics *fast*. I have never seen an accounting department that was free of politics. Realistically, any time two people work side by side, there will be some semblance of a power struggle as they try to figure out what each wants from the relationship.

In any corporation, work standards are set at the top. If you don't conform, your chances for promotion will be slim or nonexistent, no matter how hard you work. The work must conform to what management wants, not what *you* think management would like. Many times what you think management wants is distorted by your own biases. Many accountants are very productive, but not in the style your superior prefers.

Have you ever thought or said, "My boss does not appreciate me, no matter what I do." If the answer is yes, then your office politics grade is probably none too high. You need to find out from the boss, or from other subordinates, what pleases him in an employee.

You must develop your skills in making deals and negotiating. You may have to resort to compromise instead of insisting on getting your own way. You should learn how to obtain respect from the people you work with. You must learn to blow your own horn even if you aren't comfortable doing it. Who ever said you must feel comfortable in order to get ahead?

When I was younger I used to think that my boss knew exactly how good I was—he should know me by now. But I never learned how to let him know I was good. One of my biggest surprises came when the boss I thought disliked me gave me one of the biggest raises I ever got working for this large firm. Although the chemistry wasn't there, I knocked myself out on any assignment I did for him. Years later, I found out he treated everyone just as he treated me—coldly. I really learned a lesson. That was his style, and that was the way he wanted it to be, but no one had ever told me. Ask questions about your superiors, perhaps of other subordinates who have worked for the same boss. Find out how your boss likes to get things done.

One of my managers at this large corporation was nicknamed "the silver fox." He had about 30 analysts working in this department, with four supervisors. We all sat outside his office, but in full view of him. With the exception of his supervisors, if the silver fox called you by your first name, it was commonly known that you were "in." He probably did not call more than four staff people by their first names. He either called out "You!" as he pointed his finger, or snapped his fingers in your direction. Since I was the best go-fer in his department, he was forced to learn my first name.

When I left the company to become corporate controller of a smaller firm, the silver fox was visibly shaken. He really thought my greatest asset was being an outstanding go-fer, one he would find hard to replace. There were many people trying to get my job.

4

TAKING CHARGE OF SMART TIME

☐ IDENTIFY YOUR MOST PRODUCTIVE TIME

As I mentioned in Chapter 3, try to do your most important work when you are sharpest. Wise utilization of time can be a valuable asset and a strategic weapon in goal attainment. Determine when you generally feel the best, or most productive, during your company's regular work hours.

If you feel most productive before 9:00 A.M., all the better. You can take advantage of this new knowledge to create a new game plan for your career that could mean the difference between potential superior and ordinary performance.

If you have never thought about your best or most productive time, now is the time to start. Make "dollar" time work for you instead of wasting it on "penny" activity. You can begin by keeping a record of your feelings for 10 workdays. Don't worry about being completely accurate; these are meant to be rough estimates and to serve only as a broad guideline. On a scale of 1 to 10, as shown on the worksheet in Exhibit 4.1, keep an hourly record of your feelings throughout each workday. You can record this information during lunch hour or shortly after 5:00 P.M. If you are really pressed for time, then do the posting at home, at your leisure. After two weeks of posting your activity level, analyze your performance. You will probably get some idea of your strongest times.

It is also possible that you have no high points. If so, you could be in trouble—or you may just be too tough in your grading. If

EXHIBIT 4.1. Hourly Record of Feelings

Productivity Reading

Productive Factor	Before 9	A.M. 9–10	10–11	11–12	P.M. 12–1	1–2	2–3	3–4	4–5
Energy									
Concentration									
Drive									
Motivation									
Confidence									
Total									

Date _____ 198___

1. Lousy
2. Bad
3. Acceptable
4. Below average
5. Average
6. Above average
7. Very good
8. Excellent
9. Superior
10. Walk on water

so, wait a few weeks, then begin keeping records again and reanalyze your activity.

After you have established some parameters for your best hours, read the next section to learn how to utilize your findings.

☐ SCHEDULE "SMART TIME" FOR DECISION MAKING

If you say you have no control over your time, because of meetings with your boss, emergencies, constant phone calls, subordinates' needs, and so on, you are not alone. The typical manager is interrupted 6 to 9 times per hour and receives 30 to 40 phone calls a day. That's one reason many people arrive at the office early and work late—to avoid the telephone. If you allow office interruptions to control you, you will be subjected to a career in which your priorities are dictated by others.

If you discover that you feel sharpest between 7:00 and 9:00 A.M., use some of this time for your most important work—decision making. (Certainly there would be no meetings at 7:00 or 8:00 A.M.) You may have to change some old habits. At that early hour you are probably enjoying your second cup of coffee, or reading the comics, sports page, or fashion page. You may have to sacrifice and leave home earlier than usual. Is this important to your success? Think about it seriously. This may be the best time to be at work, to read over and study directives from the top, to review complicated proposals or contracts and difficult tasks. If you have a private office, close your door. If not, you'll just have to concentrate more. Besides, you won't have as many distractions this early in the morning. This is the ideal time to plan and review your schedule for the day, particularly if you have discovered that you are a morning person. If the boss requested a project report from you on a certain day, but didn't specify the time, then you opportunistically schedule it for your quality time. That way you will show your highest quality productivity. If you have thought about meetings that are geared to motivate staff, set them up for your sharp time.

If you know that, for example, 3:00 or 4:00 P.M. is your worst time—when you begin yawning, lack pep, and may be mentally fatigued—then, if possible, try to make yourself unavailable at that time. A walk and a coffee break may do the trick, or get into less demanding work for a little while. You have high-priority activities and low-priority, time-wasting ones. Try not to schedule low-priority items during a high-quality time slot, and vice versa. For low-quality time, keep a list of secondary activities in mind—routine letter writing, reviewing manuals, or other tasks that require little concentration and effort.

Most people waste smart time because they have not developed specific uses of their mental energies. There are two major time-wasters, external and personal. The external ones include:

Breakdown in communication

Unscheduled phone calls

Unscheduled visitors

Untrained subordinates

Lack of systems and procedures

Bureaucracy

Personal fraternizing

The personal time-wasters include:

Lack of planning

Procrastination

Unclear priorities

Poor delegation of authority

Lack of talent

Emergency management

Excessive personal phone calls

We set the pace for the day by the way we handle our first hour. Many people wastefully use this first hour to have coffee or chat with co-workers. But if you get to work early, beat the rush hour, and get a good parking place, you develop enthusiasm and momentum. The important thing is not that you come in early, but what you do with the extra time when you do come in early.

The night before, just before you leave the office, plan specific, high-priority problem solving for your first hour.

There are several questions you should ask yourself before embarking on a specific task:

1. Does this task serve a desired company purpose?
2. Should you perform this task, or is it better to delegate it?
3. What is the most efficient way to do this task?

There is no valid reason that good accountants cannot be continually on top of their job; efficient, confident, secure, happy in their work; and extremely effective, whatever echelon they occupy. But there are many accountants who, unfortunately, are at their mental peak at the wrong time. They are evening or night people, who have the most energy and enthusiasm during nonworking hours. Their thermostat appears to be working in reverse. This is why they never develop their skills properly, and don't act or sound too smart during the day.

If you are lucky enough to get a second wind in the evenings, in addition to good daytime feelings, then you have the potential to be a "super producer." This would be an ideal situation.

Time is an asset that we cannot afford to waste. Ten wasted minutes a day add up to a work week and a half in the course of a year.

What is wasting time? It's spending your working hours neither in work nor in play—talking idly, staring at nothing, procrastinating before beginning an assignment. Habit and custom lure us into many wasteful practices. Most businesspeople read their newspapers before settling down to the important challenges of the day. They use up their freshest hour in routine, nonproductive activity. Why not, instead, plan that period for constructive activity directed toward some important accomplishment?

☐ UTILIZE VISUALIZATION TECHNIQUES

Dr. Leonard Portner, who currently hosts the "Ask the Doctor" radio program on WXYT in Detroit, often discusses using "visualization techniques" for healthier living. Using these techniques in managing your career can pay big dividends in physical and mental health.

Imagine you are manager of general accounting and the next step in your career game plan is to become plant controller. The person in that position, in your opinion, is ambitious and promotable. Your guess is that it is only a question of time before he moves on and up or out. Your competitors are the managers of costs and budgets. Your plan is to position yourself so that when the job is vacant, you will be ready to step in. You can develop the following visualization techniques:

1. Imagine you are sitting in the plant controller's chair and you are in charge of all the accounting functions. This may seem strange to you at first, until you find out that it can work. What you are doing is trying out his chair (your objective) for size and fit. Visualization is like constructive daydreaming. Without a career dream or plan, you have no goal and little incentive other than salary.

Obviously this technique will not work if you are not technically qualified for the job. It will not work if your goal is unrealistic—if, say, you are aiming for the corporate controller's position as your next immediate step.

Repeat this mental image of yourself sitting in that chair while you are in the shower, in bumper-to-bumper traffic, waiting at the checkout counter of the supermarket or department store, jogging, and so on.

The conscious mind is the one you are aware of—you use it all the time in making decisions and analyzing and solving problems. Like a computer, your subconscious mind stores all the data you put into it. It actually performs a far greater function than the conscious mind. Whatever you program or store in the subconscious will control every aspect of your life. Therefore, if you program positive affirmations like "I can do it" or "I can supervise," so that they are repeated over and over again in your subconscious mind, doesn't it follow that your subconscious mind will eventually take over those affirmations? Absolutely. Again, your subconscious affirmations must be reasonably possible under prevailing and foreseeable future conditions.

2. Physically sit in the plant controller's chair, actually testing it for comfort and fit. (Make sure your boss is out of town when you do this.) It's like taking a car out of the dealer's showroom for a ride before buying it.

3. Study the plant controller's responsibilities. If you have not committed it to memory by now, obtain a copy of your superior's job description. Your company manual may spell it out in detail.

4. Build a personal mini-reference library on the controller's function, then study the books' contents regularly.

5. Observe, then study, your boss's character and mannerisms. If he is generally held in high esteem, and you like him, then it will be easier to emulate him. If he works late, it will be a good idea for you to do so. If he arrives early, so should you. This will impress him, and at the same time you are throwing out signals. These are some of the sacrifices you should be making if you want to beat out your competition to get the job you want.

6. Concentrate on doing the best job you can in your present position. This will keep your enthusiasm and energy level up. It will also make your boss look good, and perhaps help him get promoted sooner. This approach won't hurt your own chances for promotion when the right time comes. You will also feel better and even, most likely, healthier.

7. Visualization, once learned, must be a continuing process. Otherwise you will revert to your old habits, and the good effects of this unique technique will be lost.

After I became the corporate controller I wanted to be, I needed a maintenance program to sustain myself. I don't know of any executive who hasn't had self-doubts about past decisions or projects. From what many successful executives have told me in private interviews, this is a normal feeling.

One CFO confessed that every morning, in front of the mirror or in the shower, he would use visualization, repeating over and over perhaps a hundred times, "I am a good CFO, I am a great CFO." This was his habit for almost six months, until he became fully confident in his belief. His subconscious mind did wonders for him. Whatever you plant in your subconscious, you are likely to reap, providing your natural talents do their jobs efficiently.

My greatest dream came true when I became a corporate controller of a medium-sized multiplant manufacturer. This was quite a feat, since I was enjoying my comfort-zone existence as a financial analyst with a large corporation.

Early in my controllership position, I realized that supervising a corporate staff of 15 plus 6 plant personnel was not easy, particularly since I had never supervised even one accountant. What a challenge! Sure, during World War II, as a petty officer aboard a U.S. naval destroyer, I had supervised three other radiomen. But this was different. Had I bitten off more than I could chew? Again, I resorted to visualization, only this time the phrase was "I am a good supervisor." For six months I repeated that phrase 100 times a day. It worked. The combination of visualization and my determination to become a good supervisor resulted in a successful outcome. For the next 15 years of my accounting career, and later on in my consulting career, I used new visualization messages whenever I had doubts about my own abilities. I quickly learned that the problems of controllers and other financial executives never end, they just change in context. Although I didn't realize it at the time, I had spent nine years at the same corporation preparing for this position. My assignments in cost, pricing, budgets, and capital investment analysis were highly analytical.

In today's market and the coming market of the 1990s, the middle management accountant with cost/profit consciousness and instincts will become very valuable to top management. Being a good general accountant with record-keeping talents only will not be enough for those who aspire to the better, more competitive financial positions.

If you want to treat visualization as a game, fine. I have enjoyed this "sport" for the past 30 years, and I'm still having fun doing it. What's more, you are never too old to begin using visualization. Now, I hope, writing may become my third career—as I visualize it.

Effective visualization demands that you actually see the conditions you'll be facing and picture what you will have to do to make things work out well. If you don't think about what you should do, you are at the mercy of the environment. By thinking the situation through beforehand, you program yourself so that you can push the right buttons and increase your chance of succeeding.

There are many ways in which you can apply visualization to accounting. Try this technique next time you ask for a raise.

First ask yourself: Why do I deserve a raise? Think of your strengths, because you are making the assumption that you deserve a raise. Once you've got your justification clear in your mind, think through the characteristics of your superior. How do you expect him to deal with the raise issue? Then ask yourself: Given your boss's characteristics and your own rationale for a raise, what is the best interaction style? Remember, it's not simply content that counts, it's how you make your case.

Now, using visualization, prepare the scenario. Imagine walking in the door and sitting down. What does your posture look like? What might you be wearing? What do you say? Picture the room, and visualize the time of day. Then rehearse how you're going to get your request for a raise across.

When you use visualization, it's as if you're the writer, director, and producer of a play. And, if you actually go through the process in your mind, you will have set the stage for success.

☐ DEVELOP WORK HABITS THAT WILL LAST A LIFETIME

Our habits are learned, not inherited. It follows, therefore, that our habits can be unlearned.

The best time to develop good career habits is in the early stages of your career. If you were fortunate enough to have the parents, friends, and teachers who were instrumental in molding positive habits in you, while you were maturing, then many of your good habits have already been formed, and will need less attention now.

Few of us, however, grew up with the idea of developing productive habits specifically geared for the accounting field. Is it too late for you to change now? Absolutely not. Poor habits can be changed, and good habits can be nurtured and maintained. It just takes self-discipline and self-management.

Most of my accounting applicants agree that college did not prepare them psychologically or personally for maximum development in their careers. The reason some accountants flounder and never attain their full potential is that they have developed poor mental work habits over the years. How can we know what job demands will be thrown at us in the future?

Don't Become a Prisoner of Detail

Excelling at details and meeting deadlines is commendable, but don't overdo it. Take the career of "Fred Jones," an Ivy League school graduate with an MBA. In his mid-twenties he was thrust into a division financial manager's position with a large auto manufacturer. He impressed me at first because he looked and acted intellectually sharp. He had piercing eyes, a fine vocabulary, and plenty of confidence. He was good at researching, collecting, and consolidating information, and at making figures balance. But there was one flaw, a powerful one. "Fred" and his staff would spend hours, even days, trying to balance books that were off by only a few cents or dollars. It would have been wiser to contribute the few dollars from his own pocket in order to force a balance which, after all, totaled millions of dollars.

Fred's staff members constantly complained about the wasted time spent on tracing nonessential data to meet Fred's standards of perfection. Although Fred Jones kept that job for several years, he never rose any higher in that company or any other, even during a period of tremendous growth in the auto industry, with many opportunities open to the well educated and talented. Not only did Fred Jones not grow, he actually declined in status and responsibilities over the years. He was never able to change his one bad habit. Even in conversation, it took him 15 minutes to say what could have been said in one minute. He was simply too detail-oriented.

The lesson: Being overprecise is all right for clerical workers, bookkeepers, junior accountants, analysts, and teachers—but not for future controllers and financial executives.

Time Hoarding

In my 15 years in accounting, I have found only a handful of accountants who viewed time hoarding as an important factor in their career development. Those who did eventually progressed further, since they were also good at all other aspects of their profession.

What is *time hoarding?* Time hoarding simply means time management—in essence, learning to manage yourself as you switch off one habit with another. Like other habits, time hoarding can be developed. Each time you improve your time-hoarding habit, you should reward yourself. This gives you the incentive for changing bad habits that may be difficult to break.

I can remember falling into the trap of loafing when I was on the corporate controller's staff at a large corporation, at a time when my department was overstaffed. In those days, the best financial analysts were promoted to the corporate staff, where, in many cases, they were left to vegetate. For a short time, the job was heaven—little to do, with excellent pay and benefits. Some staff members even bragged to outsiders about the snap jobs we had.

My long-term goal, to become controller, was virtually shattered. There was no place for me to go. I was forced to use my ingenuity just to survive. The staff was like a country club. I grew thoroughly bored with inactivity, as did some of my equally ambitious associates. Since we had a surplus of time, we could not practice time hoarding. This atmosphere was prevalent not only in our department, with a staff of 30, but also throughout some of the other departments of the corporate staff. Many people enjoyed this arrangement and adjusted to it promptly. But years in this kind of environment did little to prepare them for competitive activity.

One enterprising fellow worker would go off and take personal courses at a local college, on company time. He also took in movies at his leisure. This went on for the four years I spent on the corporate staff. He is still with the corporation but has changed his work habits to survive.

Time hoarding means putting in 40 hours of productive effort in 40 hours of designated work time.

What wastes the most time for workers? The top time-wasters are as follows:

Meetings   15 percent
Phone calls   11 percent
Paperwork   7 percent
Travel   6 percent
Office gossip   4 percent

Meetings

Being aware of these time-wasters is the first step toward changing your bad work habits. If you are an average worker, you probably waste 50 percent of your work time. Attack your bad work habits one at a time. Do you, for example:

1. Participate in your superiors' meetings that you deem are wasteful?
2. Supervise meetings that may be wasteful, but you don't realize it?

Since time is money, too much potentially productive time spent on meetings can be wasteful of company money. How do you get around it? First, you have to be sure you are right. Second, you must know exactly what is wrong. Perhaps the boss doesn't stick to a written agenda, or goes off on tangents, making it difficult for you to help solve company problems.

If you think in terms of what's good for the company, it's up to you to discuss the situation discreetly with the boss. You should plan out a suggested agenda for your boss to use, but be reasonably sure he's not going to throw you out of the office. Perhaps you can volunteer to put the agenda together. If these ideas don't work, participate in the meetings as before, but make polite suggestions to keep things on track, without making waves or initiating boss–subordinate conflict.

If it's your meeting, stick to the format religiously, even if you don't cover the entire agenda. Place the most pressing items at the beginning of the agenda in case you run into a time problem. Have a time limit and adhere to it. Have you been meeting weekly out of habit or custom? Perhaps a biweekly meeting will accomplish the same objectives—and save precious time.

Encourage opinions from those in attendance, even if the dialogue is full of negative information you don't want to hear. It could be relevant. A one-way meeting, in which the CFO or manager does all the talking with no staff input, could be disastrous to the objectives of the meeting and the company's profitability. An exchange of views and ideas is what a meeting is all about. Realize that you don't know everything, and that other staff people are knowledgeable too.

Donald E. Peterson, chairman of Ford Motor Company, says, "The game is never won or lost by one person, but rather a composite of the group effort." In 1986, under his leadership, Ford broke all kinds of records. The company initiated cost reductions and belt tightening, and made appropriate design and accounting staff adjustments. Thousands of employees had to improve their work habits and attitudes. They had no choice.

Phone Calls

Without the telephone, business activity would come to a standstill. Yet too many unnecessary phone calls can rob you of the efficiency you need to be competitive in vying for the next rung of the career ladder.

Make sure at least 90 percent of your telephone dialogue is relevant to the operation of your company. Learn how to cut off a time-waster over the phone, but politely. It's your valuable time that is being wasted. You are always in a position to guard your precious time, if you want to. It's easy to listen to associates or even bosses who are entertaining, but are not adding to your productivity. It takes more courage to say you have another call, an approach that will curtail the time-wasting phone calls.

Although most companies have no policy against personal calls, many companies would like to eliminate such calls. If they did so, they might have a minor revolution on their hands. With dual-career families, personal calls are both necessary and desirable. Dual employment produces additional income, which leads to happier families—and happier employees.

Some companies view normal personal calls as fringe benefits and let it go at that. You can have your secretary or assistant screen out specific time-wasters—politely, of course. I know of one financial executive who uses a three-minute timer on all his calls, with the exception of calls from the president and his immediate supervisor.

Paperwork

Devise a simple, workable plan to burn through the mass of external and internal paperwork. Depending on the nature of your business and your position, paperwork may be a problem. Usually, the more complicated your responsibility, the higher your pile of paperwork. It's imperative that paperwork moves rapidly and smoothly to its final destination.

Paperwork waste is spreading through the business workplace. Fifty to seventy percent of all work hours put in by white-collar employees are wasted on paper shuffling. White-collar workers push more and more paper while taking less and less action. White-collar productivity has increased just 4 percent in the past 20 years. It's not surprising that all across the United States, top management is taking a closer look at middle management and its vast wasteland of paperwork.

You can control the flow of paper within your jurisdiction. You can reduce to a minimum the paper you want your department to work with. Obviously, this does not work for areas like payables and receivables as well as it does for high-level accounting positions. Following are some suggestions for paperwork control:

1. Screen selectively. This requires a good secretary or assistant and a good screening plan. My able secretary swiftly and accurately disposes of all incoming daily mail, assigning and distributing letters, résumés, newspapers, and magazines to the

various recruiting specialists and reviewing and processing all incoming résumés and job orders.

2. Dispose of junk mail immediately. I move the wastebasket closer to the mail. Don't bother tearing it up—that takes time and effort.

3. Use stick-on tags for instructions. Review all personal business letters and read them once. Immediately place brief instruction stickers on each letter or piece of literature ("review," "discuss," "hold," "file"). Dispose of junk letters.

4. Paper and magazines can be tremendous time-wasters. I make it a habit not to read or browse through the *Wall Street Journal,* the *Michigan Bar Journal,* the *CPA Journal,* the *NAA Bulletin,* or any other industry periodicals during work hours, especially in the morning (my most productive period). I read specific newspapers in the rest room regularly. I call this dual utilization of time. I also use "dead" waiting time (supermarket and department store lines, dentists' and doctors' offices) to read newspapers and magazines.

Years ago, I took a much needed reading course, where I learned to read faster and improve my comprehension. There I developed a habit of reading headlines and phrases of the first and last paragraphs of major articles. If your staff sees you reading newspapers on company time, it's easy for them to justify doing the same. When the newspapers and magazines stack up, I take them home and skim through them while watching sports on TV. I read with concentration only on relevant items.

Although our staff reads trade magazines during business hours, I'm not crazy about the idea. I do, however, underline and highlight any information I want staff members to read because it pertains to their responsibilities. This gives them a chance to use their time independently and, at the same time, learn more about our industry. Achievers know whether or not they have the time to participate in this exercise.

5. Concentrate on important mail. You now have a stack of mail reduced to a workable number of high-priority communications. Review, study, and write stick-on notes to remind you of the proper action. Forget your speed reading when reviewing impor-

tant data. If mail requires discussion with other people, do so swiftly before disposing of it. If you have a higher priority assignment or activity, consider delegating the letters for assignment to your staff. You can take control and direct your habits by patiently and skillfully making daily minor adjustments.

Travel

Much business travel is not really warranted. Often, a conference call could easily answer questions or solve problems requiring input from a variety of people at different locations. When considering the need to take a trip on company business, if you are cost- and time-conscious, just ask yourself: Is this trip really necessary? Answer honestly, without rationalizing. Many trips are little more than ego-lifting fringe benefits.

Office Gossip

This is a subject that can take up a book. No directive or procedures can ever totally stamp out office gossip. In fact, much accurate information is transmitted through this traditional medium. The question is whether you should foster office gossip by passing it on. It can stop with you if you choose. This will not help your popularity, but it will reduce time-wasting. You can keep gossip from spreading by not being the subject of the gossip.

Most people claim they have too much to do, and spending quality time on idle gossip only makes things worse.

Fly in Formation

The desire for individualism on the job is very strong in many accountants. They stand out like a sore thumb among all others who have conformed to company needs and standards. You may like to think of yourself as an eagle who wants to fly high. In a corporate environment, there's nothing wrong with flying high as long as you fly in formation.

I doubt that you will ever find a chapter on "individualism" in any company systems and procedures manual. Yet individualism does exist. Some individuals do not follow company rules of conduct or dress. Such a person in an office where everyone wears proper business attire, may wear a colorful sports outfit, arrive at work a little late, and take many "sick" days. In meetings this person will push for more liberal rules.

It takes maturity to become a team player. What would a manager do if you were playing baseball and didn't follow the rules? If you purposely ignored the signals of the manager, there would be chaos. You exhibit individualism in your personality and creativity in your approach to solving problems and suggesting new and better ways of doing things.

Working in a corporate environment is not supposed to be a fifty-fifty proposition. A corporation is not a pure democracy—don't expect it to be.

No one admires the accountant who can't make up his mind or is swayed by every stray opinion he hears. Strong decisions, based on logical reasoning and taking a reasonable risk occasionally, are the signs of an eagle flying in formation.

Every accountant has something personal to give to the job and the company. The "average" person exists only on paper, in charts and surveys. No one is really "average." You are unique, with qualities and abilities all your own. When you think about the job you have and the job you really want, you must also think about the person you are now and the person you want to become.

I have know many "yes men," but none of them ever admitted it or even were aware they were considered yes men by others. Such people erroneously label themselves "company men" or "loyal employees." They prefer not to rock the boat, ever. They prefer not to deal with the consequences of challenging someone.

Workaholics: The Good and the Bad

The Good.   It's very difficult to pinpoint a workaholic accurately. It's especially difficult to distinguish a dedicated worker from a true workaholic. I believe in working conscientiously, with heavy mental concentration. Noise, laughter and discussion around me seldom distract my thought process from 9:00 to 5:00. I developed this work habit; I did not inherit it. Yet I take four week-long vacations every year, for relaxation and stress avoidance. I don't consider myself a workaholic, since I believe I virtually do 45 hours of work in the space of a traditional 40-hour week. I enjoy working hard and making every minute count.

The Bad.   How do you become a workaholic? First, you have to love your job too much; second, you have to have so much fear of losing your position that you are obsessed with your job. Your home and family life have diminished dangerously. Your children or spouse are neglected, and your spouse may even be considering divorce unless you spend more time at home. Third, your devotion to work is compulsive, irrational, and usually unproductive and unhealthy. Yet we hear of many self-admitted workaholics who sacrificed almost everything to gain success. Many corporations would not have survived if it were not for the self-proclaimed workaholics whose drive and zeal made things work. Before you choose to become a workaholic, however, decide whether it is worth it.

How to Handle Time-Wasters

We are all victimized by fellow employees who enjoy chatting and make us waste time while attempting to avoid working themselves. That's a 200 percent time loss to the company—nothing to sneeze at. Don't let these time-wasters trap you. Time is a precious commodity. The following are a few tips that work for me:

1. Avoid eye contact. Look the other way or cross over to another aisle when you know a time-waster is about to corral you into a long one-sided conversation. If you make eye contact, it's usually a sign for him to initiate a conversation.

2. Learn to say no without actually saying no. Politely and honestly say you're working on an emergency project and would be happy to talk to the person later—much later.

3. If you are in a room and the time-waster is blocking the doorway, so you can't escape, so be it. Give him a minute—then literally *run*.

4. When you are up against a deadline and someone drops in

with lower priority information, use the stand-up routine. Get up, make a gracious remark about how busy you are, then walk the intruder to the door. If you value this person's friendship, you can always apologize when you have more time.

5. Keep on working—don't look up at the perpetrator. He will get the message without a word being spoken. If he doesn't, initiate conversation, smile, nod your head, then get back to work. Obviously, if this is your boss, you can allow more time, but remind him that he wants his assignment done on time.

There never will be enough time to do everything we want to do in our career and life. There is time for the most important things. The objective is to decide what is most important, then do it.

☐ THE PROBLEM SOLVER

The management accountants of the 1960s and early 1970s labored in an increasingly complex environment, mainly due to technological progress. In the near future, you will face an onslaught of complex problems for which you will be expected to find solutions. It is practically impossible to provide the right solutions to all your problems, but you can strive to reach the best solutions under constantly changing conditions over which you have little direct control. Computers are not a panacea for all your problems, although they may help minimize them.

This section is mainly concerned with providing a logical, orderly, open-minded guide to problem solving, as well as a quick review for those accountants who are using their own personal formula for solving everyday problems. This approach will not ensure that the correct solution will be found every attempt, nor will it guarantee a solution to every problem; however, it should make the accountant aware of the ever-present temptation to make pronouncements and arrive at hasty decisions about highly complex problems, which can actually be simplified if approached methodically.

Let's begin with the prediction that solutions to problems based on general knowledge, intuition, memory, experience, or historical facts *alone* will, in the long run, invite a catastrophe. In conjunction with a systematic plan, however, these aids can be used to advantage. The following suggested steps are listed in the order in which they should be followed, but deviations are encouraged when circumstances warrant.

1. Recognize and define the problem.
2. Accumulate all possible information.
3. Note possible solutions.
4. Examine and choose the most logical solutions.
5. Put the solution to work.

Recognize and Define the Problem

Some accountants find it difficult to believe that the most difficult part of problem solving is recognizing the problem. You are on your way to solving your problem once you can write it down and state it plainly. Problems, however, seldom come up in a clear-cut form. Usually, in a problematic situation, the symptoms are more apparent than the real malady, and can easily start you off on the wrong track, and cost your company time and dollars in putting effort in the wrong direction. That's why it is most important to identify your problems correctly.

The problem may actually be made up of a number of subordinate problems, each of which should be analyzed individually. Segregate each component and direct your energy toward the phase of the problem that is within the range of your particular position or jurisdiction. If you have gone as far as you can, and have come to a reasonable understanding of what the problem really is, *write it down*. This will provide a guide for you and any associates who may be assisting you.

Accumulate All Possible Relevant Information

Accumulate all the information that might be significant concerning your problem. If it is possible to obtain cost data, don't settle for supposition or a chance remark by a manager. Probably the biggest headache in problem solving is the question of how far you should go in getting information. The answer is always that it depends on the type of problem, how much time you have, and the scope of your position. You seldom hear of an error being made as a result of having *too much* factual information. If you keep an open mind and earnestly attempt to solve the problem, you will eventually come to a conclusion when you think you have enough information.

As you gather the facts, put them in order to assist you in making sense out of them. You can plot a flow chart or scatter chart, or draw a rough sketch or diagram of the situation. The important thing is to put it on paper. Critically analyze each item as you gather data, and always keep your mind open to such questions as:

Is the source trustworthy and reasonably correct?

Is there also a source other than the accounting department? If so, double check or compare.

Is the information received construed as absolute fact, opinion, or a combination of both?

You will be evading your obligation if you accept without careful judgment every opinion voiced by your associates or supervisors. You may have a great deal of respect for their knowledge and discretion, but if your superior is depending on you to furnish alternatives to find the solution, you owe it to him to subject his suggestion to the same evaluation for logic that you apply to all the other information. There is no better way to gather data than to get out and investigate visually yourself, since you will then be getting information straight from the horse's mouth.

Note Possible Solutions

Listing possible solutions is not as easy as it sounds—it requires productive thought. This may be a good spot for getting help from group thinking—that is, explaining to a diversified but interested group the problem or problems at hand. Individual ideas thus are brought into perspective. Sometimes this is not possible, and solving the problem is still left to the accountant. Keep an open mind, and let your imagination wander over the collected facts.

Write down all the possible solutions you can think of, even if some of them seem illogical. Do not try to evaluate at this time. The more possibilities for solving problems you have, the better your chances of arriving at the *best* solution, not merely a good or workable one. One approach to this phase, especially if you cannot come to any solutions that seem plausible, is to stop and divert your efforts to other problems. Such a change will place old problems in your subconscious mind, so that when you return to the problem, you can attack it with renewed vigor and discernment.

Examine and Choose the Most Logical Solutions

Now you can proceed to the most crucial point in your scientific analysis. This is where you must use objectivity, that is, unprejudiced and impersonal standards. Sift and test each possible solution against the same criteria; these usually can be arrived at by answering questions similar to the following:

Will this solution solve the problem partly or absolutely?

Can this solution be put into practice with a minimum of cost?

In order to institute the plan for solution, will there be serious objections because of company policy or from other departments?

Is remedying the problem worth all the effort involved?

The next step is to rate your solutions roughly in order of importance. A simple "bad," "good," "very good" grading should suffice.

Now you must decide which of the solutions is the best to solve this particular problem. Sometimes one obvious solution stands far above all others, but usually it is not that simple. It is also possible that one solution passed all the previously mentioned tests, while others were graded far down the list. The best solutions frequently result from putting together two or more of the possible solutions, taking the strong points of each. The more ingenuity and technical proficiency that can be applied to your solutions, the greater is your chance of success in solving the problem.

Some understanding of probabilities is particularly useful in making a decision. You may think that if the chances are 1 in 3 that a desired result will ensue, you can be sure of achieving it in three tries. Actually, the likelihood of the event *not* happening is twice as great as the likelihood of it happening. Perhaps you had better not recommend undertaking such a risk unless the company or department can afford the failure that is likely.

Put the Solution to Work

Now that you have worked out the best solution on paper, you must put your beliefs into practice. You may end up further revising and modifying your original plans. If the problem vanishes once the planned solution is in operation, however, you can be sure that you made the right choice. If the problem reappears even after you have adjusted the original plans, then you must take another look at some other potential solutions for guidance and project these solutions into the problem. Would another solution have been more adequate? Did you omit or misinterpret some vital information?

Retest your solution. If it does not work, redefine the problem—it may have been stated incorrectly in the first place. Go through the entire cycle again from a different point of view.

Once all these problem-solving processes have been fixed firmly in your mind, they tend to become automatic. Many smaller problems could be approached from this analytical standpoint mentally, without resorting to written notes and memos.

There will be some occasions when, because of time pressures, you cannot follow all the suggested steps. Adjust your approach to meet the situation. The important thing to remember is the steps you need to take in your plan to simplify the problem.

☐ MOTIVATION

Whose responsibility is it to motivate accountants to do great things for the company?

At times, I believe it's the company's job to motivate a potential executive. At other times, accountants are on their own and must motivate themselves.

The best-known motivators are salary and fringe benefits. However, it is apt to take bigger and bigger raises to produce less and less improvement. I believe that frequent small raises motivate employees even if only for a short period of time. Most accountants like to work. If the proper climate is provided, they will want to do a good job. This climate depends on the establishment of relevant goals in each work assignment. If accountants know what is expected of them, how their assignments fit into the total corporate effort, and why this effort is meaningful, they will be more productive. Once a job is well done, of course, what employees need is recognition from the boss.

Management should eliminate the barriers a good worker faces, such as oversupervision, a poor work environment, and inadequate tools.

Accountants should be given challenging work in which they can assume responsibility. This approach, called *job enrichment,* can include:

1. Removing some controls on employees while retaining accountability
2. Increasing the accountability of individuals for their own work
3. Giving each person a complete natural unit of work (module, division, plant area)
4. Granting additional authority to employees in their activity
5. Making periodic reports directly available to the employees themselves, rather than to their supervisor

6. Introducing new and more difficult tasks not previously handled

7. Assigning individuals specific or specialized tasks, thereby enabling them to become experts

Generally speaking, there are five factors that will motivate people to superior performance and effort:

1. Achievement
2. Recognition
3. The work itself
4. Responsibility
5. Advancement

Don't belittle workers' initiatives and achievements as being pursued only for profit. People do work for profit, to take care of their families and themselves. But they also work to enjoy the excitement and meaning that achievement provides for their own mental growth and happiness.

Motivation is a complex, dynamic area. What works in one situation will not work in another, but the aforementioned are ground rules that should be mastered.

☐ NEED FOR SELF-ESTEEM

The greatest single factor causing young accountants to leave a company is disappointment with their own prospects. Having been told, "we want you," new employees are confused if they find, 6 to 12 months later, that nobody seems to remember who they are.

Need for Respect

Often a company falls short in convincing new accountants about their early expectations. The feeling of being part of the team is just as important as salary and benefits. Motivation should be adjusted to meet the needs of the employee. In most cases, younger subordinates require different motivation techniques from more mature associates. Here, I break these categories down by age brackets.

Late Twenties (the Sophomore).   Once accountants have passed through the uncertainties of their training period, two kinds of personalities clearly arise.

1. *Cautious:* The cautious employee is the passive "company man" concerned primarily with salary and benefit programs. Old before their time, these employees are more interested in the prestige that the company and their jobs provide than in their own long-range progress. Money and status appeal to them most.

2. *Opportunistic:* The opportunist is the talented person with great energy, the kind who will work for slave wages during a recession just to get valuable long-term experience. Opportunists are likely to be married men with a family and a mortgage on a new house. They can't waste time; they must get ahead fast.

The wise manager will appeal to these opportunists by giving them different levels of responsibility each year. A large company can do this by assigning various projects. A small company, with some special effort, can also find ways of keeping young potential accounting executives interested. These employees are first-class executives in the making.

Early Thirties (the Premature Comer).   During this stage, the opportunity-minded may definitely feel that they have found the right formula. Self-confident and shrewd, these people mature rapidly and can be regarded as potential top executives. Fast promotions and a chance to learn are the best incentives for these exceptional people.

Thirty-five to Forty-five (the Experienced).   By now, rising accountants have gained valuable experience and want to capitalize on it. Maybe they are restless and yearn for greener pastures. Healthy salary increases and promotions may encourage them to stay. It is best to individualize fringe benefits so that they will not seem like the same benefits given to everyone else.

Employees of this age want a sense of individual recognition and a feeling of personally getting ahead. If money, authority, and prestige do not have the desired stimulating effect, the company may have to resort to in-depth counseling.

Newly hired employees in this age bracket should be handled carefully, too. They're ready to make some sacrifices in return for the chance they believe the new company offers. They also want and need fresh experiences. If a job or title seem a dull repetition of the past, these ambitious new employees will feel let down.

Forty-five to Fifty-five (Midcareer Executives). People in this category undergo fluctuating psychological experiences. Perhaps their children have grown and married, and their fast game of handball has gradually slowed down. Such changes are bound to affect their outlook on life.

Dependent, passive employees will appreciate new fringe benefits, imaginatively applied, and such marks of prestige as larger offices, convention trips, interesting titles, and leased cars. Greater security and longer vacations will help keep them functioning happily.

To hold and interest the truly talented people, however, an entirely different set of motivational techniques is needed. Money and security are not adequate incentives.

These financial executives, the most aggressive and the best, are no longer willing to accept company management by one person or by committee. Case after case can be cited, in banking and accounting, of people in their forties and fifties who switched companies because they were frustrated.

When top management fails to take adequate steps with these people, the pattern is usually the same: They resign and, because management knows their real worth, are then offered higher salaries if they will stay. More often than not, these people have a need to establish real records in companies that will let them take charge in their own way.

What these energetic, ambitious hotshots may also need is a

spot higher up the ladder. They should at least be given new and more challenging assignments. Sometimes that's all they want. One restless man was satisfied when he was asked to take charge of setting up a new EDP–audit department from scratch. Another was delighted to be given the responsibility for developing a flexible manufacturing budget worldwide.

Fifty-five to Sixty-five (the Older Executive).   In the last ten years before retirement—even earlier in some cases—executives begin to see the end of their business career ahead. Many people at this point decide that they want to do something significant with their lives before they retire. Others cultivate an interest in something with personal rather than financial rewards—like farming.

Inevitably, people in this age group feel a decline in their physical powers. They are likely to argue for the wisdom of taking three days instead of two on a trip. Older executives also begin to fear they are losing their influence in the organization. "How did so-and-so happen to get that promotion?" they wonder jealously. And many of them become unwilling to take risks.

In happy contrast to the people who are coasting toward retirement are those who keep their engines running full speed—the company's "prize tigers." Loaded with experience, they can make huge contributions to company progress. And supplying the right incentives can often mean the difference between the problem executive and the star performer.

Appeals to the older person's experience are likely to have a strong effect. Words like "Bill, you're the only man in the company who has knocked around with this long enough to handle it" are likely to win new efforts from the older executive. Moves that tie these older people into the center of things, such as requests for advice, are sound approaches to use at the right time.

No two accountants are exactly alike, not even in the same age bracket. The oldest person still has some motivations shared by the youngest. But it is possible to make workable plans on the basis of age. And it's clear that the motivation patterns of capable executives change subtly but definitely as time passes.

Match the motivation to the person, and chances are you will increase that executive's value to the company.

Planned Creativity

You're riding home from work, or taking a shower, when suddenly it hits you: "Hey! Why don't I . . . ?"

You've got a bright idea. It came from nowhere. You were not hunting for it. But here it is, a diamond dropped in your pocket. It's an idea for reducing costs, getting an employee to do more, solving a problem, or simplifying your job.

When will you get another idea like that? There's no telling. Bright ideas don't come often—that is, unless you know how to make them come. And you can learn how.

History is full of people who had that incalculably valuable knack. Thomas A. Edison, who started with little education, ended up with hundreds of patents and a tidy fortune. On a smaller scale, there was the employee at Remington Rand who collected 300 times on ideas he dropped into the suggestion box. These are the people who move ahead. No big company can survive long without them. One indication of the value of ideas is the $20 million given away by U.S. companies every year for employees' suggestions.

You can get bright ideas yourself, whether your goal is to impress the boss, get a better job, or just make things run more smoothly at the office. Today, the art of creating ideas is close to a science. Psychologists have analyzed it. Big companies that live on new ideas have spent millions refining it. Their conclusions:

You get bright ideas by combining old ideas in new ways.

You can improve your ability to do this without too much effort.

Concentrate on your objective, for example, reducing costs.

Think about your objective during "dead" time.

Following are seven questions to ask to trigger new ideas:

1. Can the task be done backwards? Upside down? Inside out?
2. Can you borrow an idea from some other profession?
3. Can you substitute something?
4. Can you leave something out?
5. Can you add something?
6. Can you make it bigger? Smaller? Stronger? Weaker? Heavier? Lighter?
7. Can you do it more cheaply?

As a financial accountant, you can bring up such questions when meeting with production and manufacturing management. Many times they are so close to a problem that they may not see the obvious, as an accountant might.

Procrastination

Procrastination is the most common of human failings. Putting off until tomorrow the things you should do today leaves you with a double burden. The thought of having more to do than you have time to do may induce you to do absolutely nothing, and the undone tasks pile up until they seem insurmountable. Then you may lose your temper or do something else equally irrational.

Take advantage of little bits of "found" time. When you're caught in a traffic jam, don't fret and fume. Instead, put a cassette on salesmanship into your cassette recorder, and wait out the traffic jam while learning something new or reviewing something old that you may have forgotten.You can always watch for little chunks of found time—when the train is late, or a dinner is delayed. Always have an educational paperback on hand to read.

I may have been the world's greatest procrastinator for at least half of my working life. This same self-inflicted, irrational torture probably infects 98 percent of all accountants. Almost everyone I know in my field procrastinates part of the time, though I doubt that anyone procrastinates all the time. Obviously, if you did not cater to this bad habit, you would be so successful you could not stand yourself.

As I look back at my career, some key procrastinations harmed my development seriously. I waited two years before eventually joining Toastmasters to improve confidence. I never did obtain an MBA, as I had hoped and wanted to. I stayed with one company at least five years longer than I should have, even though I knew I was in a dead-end job. I first thought about writing a book like this one over ten years ago. I had planned to write a book on how to quit smoking long before a number of books came out on this subject. I could go on and on and make myself feel guilty about all these omissions. However, I do wonder sometimes how much further I would have gone if I had solved my problems with procrastination earlier in my career.

I believe laziness and comfort-zone living was responsible. To change, we must change our habits—it's as simple as that! But it's not too simple to change a habit you are comfortable with, like smoking. How many times have you quit, only to start all over again? You must motivate yourself to do so. Fear of losing a job could motivate you to stop being late for work, or to overcome a high rate of absenteeism. Increased family financial needs could easily stimulate you to improve on your procrastination habit.

The greatest motivator of all is the reward you will obtain when you finally succeed in gaining control over procrastination. Imagine succeeding at everything you set out to do, instead of putting things off until a later date.

5

WHEN YOU HAVE REACHED A PLATEAU

Sooner or later you will reach a plateau in your career. You will face a relative lack of progress; you'll be stuck with no place to go. No college textbooks can prepare you for the dilemma you face at this point. How you react can have a lasting effect on your career. It will make a difference whether you reach your plateau early, in midlife, or late in your career. Your age and how long you have been with the company, as well as your position there, are important too.

With middle management belt-tightening accelerating, by the 1990s there won't be enough higher level finance jobs available. Also, the pyramid factor begins to throw resistance in your path, as you compete for fewer and fewer executive jobs. Ninety-nine percent of all managers will reach a plateau.

Goal-oriented people will identify the plateau much sooner than those who lack ambition or have no long-range plan. Those who think in terms of their comfort zone may not be eager to admit to themselves that they have stopped growing. Many can't even recognize the symptoms. I have listened to descriptions of hundreds of symptoms of "plateauing." The following are the most common ones:

1. You haven't had a merit raise in two years (assuming there was no salary freeze in effect).

2. You haven't had a promotion in five years.

3. Less experienced peers are getting the more important assignments.

4. You feel you are in a rut—you can do your job in your sleep.

5. You are no longer eager to go to work—the challenge is gone and you feel frustrated.

6. You have begun talking about retirement even though you are too young.

7. You are in the comfort zone—"out to pasture."

8. No one listens to your suggestions anymore.

9. You have not taken a self-improvement course or seminar in three years to keep up with changing technologies.

10. The quality of your work has leveled off or, worse yet, deteriorated.

11. You often say to yourself, "Is that all there is?"

12. You get "red-circled"—your job classification is downgraded, although your salary remains the same.

13. You are suffering a burnout.

14. You see an ad in the classified section that tells you your company is going outside for the job you would like to have.

Now that you have recognized the symptoms, what do you do? Decide to leave? Not necessarily. This is a critical time in your career life. But you should analyze the meaning of your situation before you react.

For example, in symptom #7—if you are in the comfort zone—you are not alone. Although most accountants won't admit being in a comfort zone, three out of five accountants fall into this trap sometime during their career. Excellent fringe benefits and regular raises during good economic times (but with no significant promotions or more challenging assignments) can cause you to become career-content—for the wrong reasons.

"Ed Bouchert" was supervisor of general accounting at a large

division of a giant manufacturing firm. He had been content, but
not happy, in that position for five years. Because of reorganization he was transferred to a nonmanufacturing division,
where he was again content but not happy for another five years.
His salary soared because of seniority, but his job appreciation
declined. Ed admitted he needed professional happiness more
than financial success. This was burnout, though no one called it
that. Ed decided to change careers and become a sales represen-
tative for a large financial planning firm. This astounded those
who were close to him and had always thought of him as a
low-key, shy, cautious individual. But Ed had hidden talents—
most of all, determination. Today, Ed is happy as a lark, doing
what he loves to do—selling stock. He succeeded by breaking his
comfort-zone habit.

As for symptom #11, "Tom Stevens" once whispered to me, "Is
that all there is?" As a financial analyst with an MBA, he had
reached a plateau at an early age despite the fact that he was
bright, energetic, and ambitious. In his department there were
at least 5 out of 16 other analysts who would precede him for
promotions for reasons of technical proficiency or seniority
alone. Tom was a frustrated young man, ready for a burnout. He
was underworked and underutilized. His job really was that of a
glorified clerk.

One morning Tom came to work beaming. He had found the
ideal job, as assistant controller with a small manufacturing
firm. Tom was very happy with his new job and was promoted to
controller after a few years. The company lost a valuable
employee by not planning better assignments for Tom Stevens—
and for many accountants like him.

Symptom #13 is burnout.

"Hank, get me out of here," were the first words spoken to me
over the phone by "Edwin Carruthers," group controller of a
five-plant metal-stamping operation. At age 41, Ed had all the
symptoms of a temporary burnout. I've witnessed hundreds of
similar cases in the past 16 years. Although his salary was
$65,000, plus a $10,000 annual bonus, he wanted me to find him
a $40,000 accounting job that did not have the pressures he was
experiencing. He wrongly reasoned that a lower salaried job

would offer less stress and would consequently solve his immediate problem.

I counseled Ed very cautiously since I sensed that this was a critical situation for him. I explained that there could be just as much stress and pressure in a $40,000 job as in his $65,000 job. I told Ed that his attitude toward his responsibility might be the real problem—there are no stress-free jobs in accounting. (If you do find one, it isn't much of a job.)

Shortly thereafter we met face to face in my office and discussed his malady in greater detail. Ed looked like a beaten man. His forehead was deeply wrinkled, and he had a dazed, blank stare brought on by insomnia. His voice was unnaturally high-pitched, rapid, and jerky. But after a cup of coffee and my assurance that I understood his situation and that he himself could solve it, Ed calmed down.

"Ed," I advised, "you know that a $40,000 job will not solve what ails you. First of all, your standard of living is geared to a $75,000 income. What will taking a $35,000 pay cut do to your family?"

Instead of answering, Ed poured out his tale of administrative woes. He said he'd been working a 60-hour week for the past two years, with no vacation. He was afraid that if he took time off, the whole company would fold—yet his peers, superiors, and subordinates all took vacations. Most of his assistants contributed only about 40 hours of work per week. The profit column looked good and was accepted favorably by the corporate CFO.

I offered Ed several suggestions for a possible solution:

Take an immediate vacation, if OK'd by the general manager.

Reduce his work week to 55 hours.

After two months, reduce it to 50 hours.

Begin a physical excercise program.

Delegate some of his work to subordinates, and manage his time more effectively.

I gave him a copy of Robert H. Schuller's *Tough Times Never Last, but Tough People Do!* (1983) to read on his vacation.

More than three years have gone by, and Ed is still with the stamping company, earning $85,000 with a shorter work week and regular vacations. His résumé has been transferred to our inactive file—he's no longer looking for a change.

There are basically two kinds of plateaus. In the first case, you know you have reached a plateau, and you don't mind too much—you can live with it. In the second case, you realize your career status but don't like it and are contemplating doing something about it.

During my career I experienced three plateaus—two that were unacceptable and one that I didn't mind at all.

□ AN ACCEPTABLE PLATEAU

After five wonderful, challenging years at a large division of a giant corporation, I was promoted to the corporate finance staff. I hit a plateau after about three years on the same job with no classification improvement or more challenging assignments. Although I did receive fine merit raises, and my stock option plan multiplied, I sometimes wondered why. I knew I was worth the salary, but I didn't feel I was earning it from the amount of work I was given.

I accepted this period of no progress because of the excellent fringe benefits and the comfort zone in which I suddenly found myself. My career ambition was frozen. I enjoyed my situation, sort of, for three years. In reality, I was rationalizing. I was around 39 years old when I realized that my attitude toward this career plateau was changing from enjoyment to boredom. At that point my situation changed from an acceptable to an unacceptable plateau. I became concerned that time was passing me by, and I began a plan to do something constructive about it. But my talk with the personnel department proved fruitless.

Don't be fooled by rationalizing and accepting a plateau. Don't say:

1. I'd like to quit, but I'm too old.
2. Things are not going to change, so I might as well get used to it.

3. I might just as well do as little as possible—after all, why kill myself?
4. I would consider a change, but my family comes first. They depend on my income.
5. It's a secure job, despite my boredom.
6. I'll wait till I retire—then I'll enjoy life.

☐ AN UNACCEPTABLE PLATEAU

Many middle management financial executives find their careers blocked or at a dead end, and they don't like it. They don't accept the status quo. But before they decide to do anything about it, they must first find out:

1. Why did it happen?
2. Was it your fault?
3. Was it the company's fault?
4. What is an alternative plan of action?

For question 1, "Why did it happen?", I offer the following example. With "Ned Hudspeth," a partner with a medium-sized local CPA firm, it was a case of not recognizing that his firm was not growing at a sufficient pace in order for him to grow financially and in terms of responsibility. His original plan was to work there until retirement, but he realized after 14 years with the firm that he was at a dead end. I agreed with him— there was nowhere for him to grow with his firm. At 38, Ned realized he had reached his peak in public accounting. He reasoned that the Big Eight firms would not be interested in him because his grades from a nonrated college were too low, his salary was too high, and it had taken him three attempts to pass all the parts of the CPA exam. His appearance was excellent. He was tall and lean, and a fluent communicator, who knew his field. I had no problem finding him a fine CFO position with a growing $30 million sales manufacturing firm.

"Was it your fault when your company asked you to take early retirement?" was the question I asked "George Meyers" in an interview. He said no, but I knew otherwise—we'd checked his references. It seems George had a long financial/administrative career with a Big Three auto company. His job took him into the inner sanctum of the management elite. After 25 years, at age 56, George was asked by the company to take early retirement. He easily could have contributed another 7 to 10 years, and he really wanted to.

Mr. West, his immediate superior, said that George's record would have been excellent except for one shortcoming—a serious one. His bad habit was one that many financial executives have a difficult time coping with: knowing when to let go, even when you think you are right, when the company committee has voted just the opposite. George had many creative ideas and was an excellent technician, who also had a clear and logical approach to problem solving. George should have progressed further up the ladder than he did; his ambition was to go all the way to the top. But George virtually made a pest of himself at important executive meetings, constantly challenging decisions that had already been voted on by the hierarchy. His blind persistence caused George to fight until no one would listen. His frustration grew stronger and stronger, and his overzealous confrontations became more frequent. Sometimes he forced executive meetings to stall when it would have been prudent to let them continue. Knowing when to shut up is an art that only the select few have mastered.

You can hit a plateau at any stage of your career. Ask yourself, "Was it the company's fault?" I was 28 years old when I reached a plateau only three years into my accounting career. The Frantec Corporation was a nice place to work. Turnover was unusually low, and no one seemed to work too hard. Yet management maintained a good rapport with the staff. I had already mastered the cost accounting position of the small research and engineering plant, and things had become routine. I could easily have been content to coast, but my ambition got the best of me. Nothing worthwhile was happening to my career—and no one seemed to care. My job had no job description or classification that I was aware of; it had been handed down by the previous occupant. My boss was not aware I was losing interest in the job, nor did I let him know. I believed that since the company didn't know, it also didn't care. Instead, I should have calmly and confidently informed my boss of my feelings, rather than beginning a confidential search for a new and more challenging job. The company and I both made mistakes in judgment.

Do you have an alternative plan of action when you discover you have reached an unacceptable plateau? "Chuck Drummond" was a supervisor at a Big Eight CPA firm when he realized that there were at least four other supervisors fiercely competing for the one manager's job, which was to open up in two to three years. Realizing he had peaked, Chuck analyzed the other four competitors' background, skills, and potential. He considered himself third best and wasn't about to wait to be passed over. Although he was aggressive and ambitious, he had alternative plans. One was to join another Big Eight CPA firm. He interviewed with three others in the Detroit area, only to find his paths to the manager's position would be just as slow, although he could pick up another $2,000 to $3,000 in base salary. But Chuck would have to develop new friends and associates, and learn to deal with different bosses; it was not worth it.

Chuck's alternative plan was to find a managerial job in industry, which he quickly did. His gross income increased by $8,000 the first year. This, together with new hands-on management exposure in private industry, was his response to hitting a plateau. Being a supervisor in a Big Eight firm at age 28 gave his alternative plan much credibility and gave him personal satisfaction. His career went on a positive track; he may not reach another plateau for three to five years.

The mythical ideal age to take career risks is 35. Statistically, at this age, give or take a few years, you are approaching the peak of your marketable value, your drawing power. You have reached the halfway point of life expectancy. Putting out feelers through established, reputable employment agencies can help your career. Make sure you are dealing with a mature, street-wise accountant who has already experienced what you are going through. Choose an agency specializing in accounting placement that is staffed by controllers, CPAs or CPCs (certified personnel consultants). As for going to an agency for counseling and perhaps initiating a job search, this is part of the free service offered by many such firms. The employment agency benefits in the long run, since satisfied applicants may eventually become fee-paying clients.

Some employment agency counselors are not qualified to advise financial executives about their careers. Taking poor advice seriously can actually damage an accounting career. If your counselor is sales oriented, with no appreciable accounting or counseling history, be discerning in accepting his opinions. It might even be a good idea to use one good agency for counseling and career advice, and another to find you a better job.

☐ PLAN OF ACTION

Once you have accepted the fact that you are at a plateau, and that this is a common occurrence, you are in a good mental position to come up with a plan. The plan can result in action or in no action at all. Either choice may be good for you, depending on your personal life, skills, determination, objectives, and age. At this point, in fact, age is probably the most important factor.

Honest Talent Evaluation

Whether you like it or not, you will find it most difficult to evaluate yourself, particularly if your career is not moving at the pace you want. It is imperative that you be reasonably accurate in grading yourself. In order to handle a plateau effectively, you must have or be capable of acquiring the talent to move up another rung on your career ladder. If you lack the proper talent, or don't believe you can acquire the needed talent, then your possible moves after reaching a plateau are limited or nonexistent.

In the following, we'll assume you have reached a plateau and that you have the proper talent at various age levels:

1. *Age 28 to 34:* With at least 31 to 37 years left in your career, you should be more aggressive and risk-oriented about the strategy you will undertake when you determine that you have

peaked. You may need to inquire within your company. The most concrete information you may get will only be an impression of where you stand unless your boss is an honest and good manager who tells you to be patient, the company does indeed have plans for you. If you get a negative impression, then it may be time for you to react. You could request a lateral move, with a new boss or new division. At the same time, it would not hurt to put out "job feelers" outside your firm, to learn your marketability.

Review your last evaluation by your superior to find out your shortcomings and consider whether you need additional technical or self-improvement courses to make you more marketable internally as well as externally.

Determine whether your company's lack of growth or poor management had something to do with your stagnant position. There may be others in your company with the same problem, and morale may be poor companywide for just this reason. You may confide in others who are in the same position.

2. *Age 35 to 45:* This is the prime age group of middle managers who will be in demand in the 1990s. It is traditionally the most sought-after age group by company recruiters. There has always been a shortage of "superior" talent in this age group, although there will always be a surplus of "good" talent. Reaching a plateau will be relatively common for those in this age bracket.

In my opinion, the odds are about 15 to 1 for a 40-year-old to make it to the top 1 percent of management. At age 45, the odds skyrocket to 45 to 1. This problem is not unique to industry. The question is what to do if you recognize that you are the one engulfed in this trap. Looking ahead, you have 20 or 30 years till retirement. Since this period is your most productive, and you are very likely most marketable on the outside, you must consider alternatives.

If you are in good health and have plenty of energy, then you may want to consider the sky the limit—to go as far as your talent will take you. The following are some alternatives:

a. Seek a job with a competitor.

b. Seek a job in a related industry.

c. Consider a consulting position.

d. Consider entrepreneuring.

e. Consider staying with the company, hoping against odds that good things might happen, despite the plateau.

f. Change your attitude, accepting the plateau but imagining that you will enjoy your work no matter what it becomes.

3. *Age 46 to 55:* This is the most sensitive age, since this is also a period in which many accountants experience a midlife crisis. Some of my applicants go through a hellish time when they do not recognize this crisis or their families are unaware. Some universities and hospitals offer noncredit courses on this subject, which should be taken by accountants and/or their spouses in their late thirties or early forties so that they can learn to recognize the symptoms and learn to cope with them.

"Ed Burlingame," after spending 30 years with the same large company, suddenly realized he had reached a plateau. At age 55 he had been at the same job (general accounting manager) for 10 years, with few raises. He was no longer asked to attend important division meetings, and he could not be transferred to other similar jobs—there were none at his level. He knew he was no longer promotable and he had just gone through a difficult divorce when he came to our agency for advice. He thought his life was over. His job was literally dead, and he had no family to come home to.

We first advised him to seek psychological help. At the same time, we suggested he enroll in a Dale Carnegie course and in Toastmasters, as well as other noncredit self-improvement courses, to help develop his confidence and self-esteem. We then suggested he meet with us again in six months. A short time later Ed decided to stay with his company. We had felt he had limited talent to rise any higher. So he changed his attitude toward his company's management, began to cooperate, and become a model employee despite his career stalemate.

Ed Burlingame, at the time of this writing, was nearing 60 years of age. He planned to retire at age 65 to Florida. He finally admitted to himself that he had reached an acceptable plateau, so that he could be reasonably happy going to work every day. In his own mind, he believed he was a success.

This should be the easiest time for you to handle a plateau. You might find the company giving you assignments that are no longer challenging. They may want to place you in good administrative positions that don't require high-level decision making of any consequence to the growth of the company.

4. *Age 56 to 65:* This is the most difficult age for most veteran accountants who have reached a plateau close to the end of their career. By this time most married people have grown children who themselves have left home. They are most likely well off; they do not have to bear the high cost of children's education and household needs.

In this age bracket, it matters how high up the ladder you have gone before you begin thinking about whether or not you have reached a plateau. If, at this age, you are a CFO, and you know you cannot become president because the president has a son he is grooming for that job already, then you may consider staying with the firm and accepting the plateau. It's not too bad to be in the position of helping to train a son on his way up. If you are vested in the company pension plan, you may think twice before seriously considering making a career change.

"Dan McAlister" was 59 years old when he decided to leave his firm. He resigned as treasurer of a machining firm that had $25 million in sales. He knew it was only a matter of time before his company, like others in a no-growth industry, would reach a point of diminishing returns. Age is not as important for executives who have succeeded in attaining high levels of income (such as a 61-year-old CFO earning $100,000 to $150,000 per year). It would be significant if at age 61 a person was still earning $30,000; such a person's job marketability would be negligible.

It's Not Necessary to Change Careers at a Plateau

If you find your career blocked or at a dead end, you don't necessarily have to leave the company and seek another job or career. You should carefully review the reason for the plateau, then decide to try to get back on the track of advancement. Emphasis should be placed on organizational goals instead of personal goals. It may take time to reverse the reality of being stymied, just as it probably took some time to reach the plateau in the first place.

Determined improved performance, in conjunction with skilled conveyance of this information to your boss, will get his attention. Your performance should be extraordinary and sincere, since you must maintain at least ordinary performance just to keep your job.

If the reason for the plateau was your abrasive personality, it may take a lot of persuasion to reverse management's thinking about your shortcoming. Developing alliances may be useful, since others who are promoted will have loyal people they can take along with them. Developing alliances is very important. Some ambitious accountants develop business friendships for politically self-serving reasons, whereas some accountants develop friendships naturally, without ulterior motives. In larger firms, developing alliances is necessary for career self-preservation, but the method you use is more sensitive. Never attempt to force an alliance; these take time if they are to be meaningful. Coffee breaks and lunch are ideal times for creating friendship with employees you don't come in contact with routinely. Joining or becoming more active in an accounting association in which your boss's boss or many of your peers are active is a fine place to begin alliances away from work. If you have ambition, one evening a month is not that great a sacrifice.

If your alliances are made with people in a higher classification than yours, so much the better. Developing friendships with your peers is also necessary because your peers may be promoted someday, and your interpersonal relationship could be important in your own movement upward. I can still remember the manager of accounting of a large automotive plant, one of the Big Three. "Frank Bellmore" was considered, in essence, a protégé of "Ed Anderson", the plant controller. As Ed moved up the ladder, so did his protégé.

Developing alliances outside the company can also help your career. Such associations as the NAA, CPA, and CIA can be ideal stepping-stones to alliances. At association meetings, seek out fellow professionals from competing companies to develop acquaintanceships that can later blossom into friendships. These friends or acquaintances will become part of your career network, to be called on eventually when needed. Exchanging technical, but not confidential, information can be beneficial from an educational standpoint. Helping an association member solve a particular accounting or management problem in which you have expertise shows class, and could prove helpful in the networking game. Becoming involved and accepting association committee assignments will accelerate your alliance development plan.

Volunteer for special assignments, or work on profit enhancement or cost reduction projects on your own time. Then show the results of your extracurricular efforts to your boss. If your boss is significantly impressed and recommends further action by top management, this could help your cause considerably.

Success Self-Sabotage

There are many intense accountants who have driving ambitions. They strive sincerely toward a particular objective, but when they approach success, they are overcome by anxieties, which cause them to self-destruct, often without knowing it. Then they resume working toward the same goal with their old persistence.

I have met many accountants who fear success. These success fearers are people who actively seek success but, at the same time, fear its consequences, for a number of reasons. Their ambivalence toward success gives rise to a series of defense mechanisms, which they initiate to avoid achievement. The most obvious aspect of this phenomenon is worsened performance. Also, the person with low self-esteem will not accept flattery from others about impending success.

"Joel Turner" had everything going for him, career-wise. He was division controller of a large multinational firm. At 35, Joel was mature, had excellent credentials, was executive in appearance, and supposedly was a good family man. At the office he seemed to do and say the right things at the right time. He was 100 percent political—yet at the worst possible time he chose to have a torrid romance with a clerical worker. This shocking news spread like wildfire through the office grapevine. Within weeks everyone, including top executives in the division, knew about this romance—and they didn't like it. Joel didn't seem to care. He confided to a close peer that even though he knew he was doing wrong, he couldn't stop himself. He seemed to want to self-destruct, even though he was forewarned by his superiors of the consequences of continuing. Without realizing it, he was choosing to fail. He was sabotaging his entire career for no apparent worthy reason, although he could have ended the affair in a month without serious damage.

In three months Joel's hot romance cooled off, and Joel was transferred and demoted to an analyst classification in a nondescript division, never to be seriously heard from again.

Some industrial psychologists believe the self-sabotage motive is a real problem, affecting many more accountants than we realize. The conditions seldom surface as dramatically as they did for Joel Turner, because the self-saboteur rarely admits or even knows of this deep affliction. Many accountants fail for any of the following reasons:

1. They don't realize that whether they succeed or fail depends entirely on the decisions they make as they step on each rung of the ladder.

2. They allow their goals to die. They give up without a real fight—they lack perseverance. When they fail to get a promotion or a raise, they throw in the towel. They feel hurt when, instead, they should seek out the reasons that someone else got the job, correct their shortcomings, and begin all over again.

3. Strangely, they may have a secret fear of the responsibility that success will require of them. For example, perhaps you really would like to be promoted to controller, but it will mean leaving your close friends in the department. It will mean harder work, more time devoted to the job, and less time for home and family or friends. It will mean developing new friends and alliances at a higher level of authority. Are you willing to pay the price? This is what scares many accountants.

4. They have a negative opinion of themselves. They don't believe they deserve to get the promotion. Therefore, they

halfheartedly exercise their responsibilities to make sure they don't get the promotion or the raise.

Outgrowing Your Job

Have you ever considered that you may be in the wrong job? If so, it may be time to review your career and move on. On the other hand, there may be good reasons to stay in your job, even if it is beginning to lose its attraction. If you feel you're reasonably satisfied at present, these evaluations may open your mind to areas you have never thought about. Before you consider making a change, however, try to develop the components missing from your present job. Then, if you fail, make your move.

Take a critical look at your job.

Are you eager to get to work every morning?

Do you feel a sense of accomplishment when the day is done?

Do the rewards and satisfaction outweigh your criticisms of your job?

Is there enough space for personal advancement?

If one or more of your answers is "no," you may be in the wrong job. The matter is worth considering, if only to prove to yourself that you are in fact in the right job. And if you are not, it would be disastrous not to make a change. Even if you are content with your job, or think you are, you should appraise your career at least once a year—on your birthday.

Ask yourself some questions:

What does your work include?

What is good about it?

What is bad about it?

Have you outgrown your job?

No one can answer these questions for you. They call for introspection.

From my years of experience as an accountant and as a personnel consultant, I will try to give you a set of realistic suggestions for figuring out whether you are in the right position. These suggestions are based on extensive research and observations over the years, as I have helped hundreds of accountants assess their current and future careers.

Before contemplating a job change, ask yourself:

Why should I want to change my position?

Your critical analysis of this question will help you determine whether you are ready for a change. If you conclude that you are, the next step will be to find out whether you will be better off or worse off in another job.

Stay or Change

You may have a strong urge to move to a job that you hope will be heaven, or close to it. But the important thing is to weigh the pros and cons of changing jobs against those of staying put, in hopes of coming up with a conclusion that favors one choice over the other.

Even if you could make a perfect decision, that would not be true for long, with all the competition available in our industry today. Both accountants and jobs are forever changing, and a job that is close to perfect for you today may be quite imperfect tomorrow.

Financial executives at your level can never find a job that matches their ideal specifications, assuming they know clearly what those needs are. There is give and take in every job. In which parts of your job are you willing to give? Take?

All jobs have both tangible and intangible elements. The value of each element changes depending on the individual. To one executive, status might be important; to another, personal satisfaction might have a higher priority. One might seek independent action, another job security. Following are some important elements to consider.

Salary. The value you place on income may require long, and perhaps mind-boggling evaluation. One person may rank it first in significance, another may grade it only third or fourth. One CFO who had always considered income to be the highest priority, reappraised his values and changed his opinion once his children were older and had families of their own. His personal financial situation was excellent, his home mortgage was paid off, and he no longer needed a large salary to sustain himself and his wife.

This CFO concluded that he most wanted to spend more time with his wife, to travel, to do more reading, to play more handball. He had worked more than 55 hours a week for over 30 years. Now, his priorities were changing. He wanted to take some of his own time back. So he left the company for a job that paid less but gave him more free time. He's much happier. If, however, in your own personal situation, compensation heads the list of priorities, then you should go where the money is.

Promotion Opportunity. Where is your career going? All the way to the top? Two-thirds of the way? How do your expectations fit in with your company's growth potential? Your own growth may be tied in with that of the company. Is the company moving up in the industry at the speed you feel it should? Are your superiors aggressive, or are they complacent? If your company is satisfied with little growth while other firms are capturing large portions of business and profits, you may be wasting your time staying.

Another factor in promotion opportunity is the number of other capable accountants who occupy steps between your present job and your ultimate objective. Ask yourself: Do you really have the capability to reach your goal? Many executives know they don't have what it takes to tackle the top job, so they settle happily for a number-two or number-three job, or even a staff assignment. These wise men are more valuable to the company than those with blind ambition who are determined to get to the top without realistically evaluating their abilities and recognizing that they simply are not qualified.

Even if you now hold the top accounting job in your company, will the company grow fast enough and go far enough for you to grow?

Your Job. Do you still get the kick you used to get from your job? Does the work still stimulate you, or do you find that what used to be a challenge is now a bore? Is your interest sagging? The most important factor to consider is this: Are all your abilities being put to good use, or are your best talents being wasted?

Do you enjoy the opportunity to travel and meet new people, or, conversely, do you dislike the fact that your job takes you away from your family too much? What about adequate thinking time? Do you have hours to burn, or not enough free time? Are you working harder than you really want to?

How does your family feel about your job accomplishments?

"Why do you want to change jobs?" I asked a controller applicant recently. He answered, "Because no one listens to me. I made good suggestions, approved by my boss—but no one ever acted on them. They are filed in Drawer G—for garbage." If this is your problem, because of superiors or a president who is less risk-oriented than you, you might consider starting your own business. Success lies not necessarily in achieving what you aim at, but in aiming at what you ought to achieve.

"Chet Kapuchinski," a degreed accountant, was a capable controller with a reasonably high salary. But the urge to own his own business was too strong for Chet. He and his wife invested their savings in a specialty furniture store in a small, exclusive shopping mall. His plan was to have his wife run the store during the day, while he "moonlighted" on the evening shift. Although his wife was a capable salesperson, she had no previous business training and did not have the necessary business acumen. The income from the business was not sufficient for Chet to leave his controller's position, and eventually he was replaced in that position by a CPA. Because he was already 55, Chet had difficulty finding another controller's position at a similar salary. Although Chet now spent more time on his furniture business, sales did not increase materially. Finally, he sold the store and went back into accounting at a much lower salary. In this case, moonlighting was not the answer to starting a new business. Chet's career hit another plateau.

Job Security.   How much does job security mean to you? Are you willing to risk personal growth? How important is your vested interest in your pension and other fringe benefits?

I resigned a secure position with a secure company, after nine years. If I had stayed on for another year, I would have been vested. I switched from a secure senior financial analyst position with a large company to a much less secure corporate controller position with a much smaller company in a risky industry. Why did I take such a chance? It was the opportunity of a lifetime, coming at a time when I was completely bored with my job.

There is very little wrong with seeking security. But consider how much it will cost you in your long-range career planning.

Personal Growth.   Recently an applicant who was a CPA, employed as a plant controller, told me that he could earn $10,000 more in annual salary by moving to a larger company. He asked my advice on making the switch. While discussing the situation, we talked about his immediate boss. I was trying to find out if there was a skeleton in the boss's closet. At that point, the applicant grew excited. His boss was great! He was learning a tremendous amount from him! I asked him if the boss had reached his plateau. Had the applicant learned all that the boss knows? "No," my applicant replied. In answering this question, he solved his own problem: He decided to stay a while longer. "In two years," he concluded, "if my earnings and promotion potential are still limited, I'll reconsider a move."

What you are learning in your present job is what makes you a more valuable employee. Is your boss helping to make you a stronger executive? This is a key indicator of what you are learning. Is having a parking space next to the president important to you? Is having a deluxe office meaningful? Is the title of assistant to the president enough to make you happy— even though you know you'll never become president?

If you must be number one, go for it, even at the risk of failing. But be sure you can recover, in case you do fail.

Status.   Status has to do with ego and ambition. If you have a large ego, you had better develop a great ambition. If you have a great ego but no ambition, forget about high status—you'll never achieve it. To fulfill your ego needs, you must be highly motivated. Once you are motivated, you may even decide to become ambitious.

If you want to be "somebody" in your company—for example, CFO or vice-president–Finance—you really have to work for it. It will never be handed to you, unless you're related to the boss. Therefore, you have to determine just how high a status symbol will satisfy you. Early in your career, you can easily say you want to become the controller, vice-president–Finance, even company president. But as the years go on and you conclude you will never make president, you may settle for being number two or even number three, or maybe less than that.

If you are number two, are you getting your fair share of recognition from your colleagues, your community, and your industry? Who is really responsible for your present job unhappiness—you or your company? In many situations, the job is not living up to your expectations because you are not living up to the requirements of the position.

Is there anything you can be doing in your present company to improve those areas that are most important to you? If the answer is "no," then you are definitely in the wrong job. It's time to move on.

6

DESIGNATED ANNUAL CAREER PLANNING DAY— YOUR BIRTHDAY

Only 3 percent of all financial professionals formulate their career plans on paper. A woefully small percentage make it to the top. My guess is that the ones who write out their plans, and keep score, are the ones who eventually reach their goals.

Happy Planning Day. So you are 29, 39, 49, or 59—it's your day. Take out your manila folder for this year—the one you put together on your last birthday. You say you don't have a folder? You've never put your plans in writing? What a shame. Apparently, you don't believe your career is important enough to devote one day out of 365 calendar days to planning it.

My suggestion is this: Acquire one manila folder for each year up to age 65. Write your birthday for each succeeding year on each one. Now you are set for the rest of your career. Then designate a career planning day, as close as possible to your birthdate. Realistically, your birth date may be taken up with a party. But if not, your actual birthday is ideal for planning.

Allow yourself some time alone to mull over what you have been thinking about. Such meditation may be a reenergizer, too.

Whether you are 29 or 59, it is imperative that you begin planning for the balance of your career. It is never too late, nor is it ever too early. Even if your company has taken good care of your career so far, don't assume this will go on forever. Suppose your company is sold or acquired, or goes into bankruptcy? In these uncertain days of acquisitions, reorganizations, and middle management squeeze, you must protect yourself and your career. Don't simply allow events to happen, without being prepared. You must exercise some control over your destiny.

☐ UPDATE YOUR RÉSUMÉ ANNUALLY

The purpose of updating your résumé annually is not to prepare yourself for making a job change, although that could be a by-product. Actually you update your résumé to show yourself, graphically, what you have accomplished since your last birthday.

If this is the first time you are attempting to do this, I suggest the following:

1. Make a copy of your last résumé.
2. Review your latest résumé.
3. Make changes or additions in pencil.
4. Have the revised résumé typed.
5. On a separate sheet of paper, list the pencilled words (the changes made).

☐ DISCUSS YOUR PERSONAL DEVELOPMENT WITH YOUR MANAGER

A good superior will take time to review your progress with you. A busy or indifferent superior may tell you to wait until your annual appraisal day, or may simply refer to your last review, or he may pick a date that's convenient for him.

If your annual review has been in writing, obtain a copy and place it in your "Designated Annual Career Planning Day" file.

If your company is too small to have formal reviews, this may be a good way to initiate one, if doing so will help the company meet its management development needs.

What questions should you bring up during your review?

Raise questions that will give you some insight into the improvements you need to make in your personal character, technical knowledge, or attitude that will benefit the department or the company. Ask questions that will give you answers on how to help the company reduce costs or improve profits.

If a particular accounting position that you were eyeing remains open for a long time, that is a tipoff that there will be organizational changes. If the boss avoids you or acts indifferent toward you while making the decision to fill this opening, it's probable that you are not in the running for the promotion. Usually dialogue and activity increases between the boss and a person who is likely to be promoted.

The following are questions you should ask during or after the review:

1. What technical skills do you need to improve?
2. What technical skills do you need in order to be promoted?
3. What personal character traits do you need to improve on your job?
4. What personal character traits will you need in order to be promoted?
5. What plans, if any, does your company have for your future?

If you are willing to relocate for the right opportunity, tell your manager or personnel department to put that on your record.

Your superior should be made aware of your aspirations. Look for signals from your boss as to whether what you expect is probable or even possible. Be aware of publicized or subtle organizational changes.

Don't discuss the contents of your career planning folder with your superior, particularly if your goals could intimidate him. If your objective is to have his job someday, you obviously don't want to say so. However, if part of your plan is to broaden your education to include certain courses that may help you on the job (e.g., Long-Range Forecasting, Modeling, Lotus 1-2-3, Symphony, MBA, CMA, or CIA), then it would be a good idea to discuss those goals.

If your career planning folder includes areas of interest that differ from your present responsibilities (e.g., general accounting duties versus industrial and standard cost interests), discussing these interests with your boss will give advance notice that you may be ready for broader responsibilities. The boss may be in a position to recommend you, should such an opening open up. Make it clear you are not suggesting you want to leave the department, but that you want what is beneficial for the company, the boss—and then yourself.

☐ HOLD YOUR RÉSUMÉ IN ABEYANCE

Having an updated résumé doesn't mean you are about to change jobs or are ready to enter the job market—far from it. Having an updated résumé is like having your car tuned up regularly so that it's always in top condition, ready to go at any time.

An up-to-date résumé is your "security blanket." It should make you feel confident about yourself and your accomplishments to date. If you are happy with the content of the résumé, it may be the stimulus you need to make changes. Your résumé is *you;* reviewing your résumé is like looking into a mirror of your career. If you don't like what you see, it may be time to make adjustments.

☐ REVIEW THE PREVIOUS YEAR

You should have a set of questions ready to ask yourself, about last year's goals and your actual performance (see Exhibit 6.1).

EXHIBIT 6.1. Reviewing the Previous Year

	Not Adequate	Adequate	More Than Adequate
Received salary increases			
Enjoyed your responsibilities			
Rapport with immediate superior			
Rapport with peers			
Self-improvement courses taken			
Suggestions made for cost reductions			

The questions in Exhibit 6.1 are by no means "gospel." You can add or change questions annually as you mature in your career.

An accountant's salary should be a barometer of performance; it should be reviewed carefully and seriously. Even if you are part of a multi-income family, your individual salary should be analyzed annually.

Are you satisfied with your salary and benefits?

Have you received a salary increase since your last birthday?

Was it adequate or not?

Do you think you contributed more than the amount of the salary increase?

Is your salary in line with industry parameters?

Is your salary in line with your job title (available in the *Wall Street Journal* or with private placement firms)?

If you are not satisfied with your salary increase, was it because of something you had control over?

Was lack of the desired salary increase due to a company freeze or to poor financial performance by the company?

Are you satisfied with your salary and benefits? If your answer is no, you can join approximately 95 percent of the accountants I have interviewed in the past 15 years. This question is the most difficult to answer honestly. Admitting being overpaid is almost impossible for an accountant's ego to accept. I have seldom heard an applicant categorically say, "I'm satisfied with my salary, but find me a job with more responsibility and challenge."

One of my subordinates once told me he needed a pay increase because it costs more money to feed and take care of his family. He never mentioned why he thought he was worth more than he was earning. You guessed it—he did not get the raise, although I did feel empathy for his personal needs.

Was lack of desired salary increase due to a company freeze or poor company performance? If the answer is no, you may have a problem worth exploring as an employee. Most professional accountants expect a reasonable annual increase if there are no extenuating circumstances (such as a recession or a freeze). If your percentage of increase is in line with that of other employees in your classification, then you need not worry about the consequence of a smaller-than-desired increase. Asking the boss for a higher renegotiated increase does not make sense, since the boss will have to admit he was wrong before coming up with more money for you. Your boss's superior will raise his eyebrows when he sees a pay increase requisition go through for a second time. If your performance and special assignments were of such a magnitude that you honestly think you really merited considerably more, then you should wonder why your superior did not agree. What do you do? You can't threaten to resign or actually quit if you don't get your way. Assuming you are under 45 years of age, you should put out job feelers to compare your salary status with that of others like yourself in the same industry. This is for your own peace of mind.

It's your attitude that is important in this situation. The fact that you were given difficult assignments in the first place should please you. The fact that these assignments broadened your experience is good for your personal development. If the assignments were difficult and complex, and you succeeded, you can put another feather in your cap. Remember, you learned more as a result of the assignments, and that adds to your marketability as an accountant should you decide to make a career change later on.

Before you even entertain the thought of making a career change simply because you didn't think your raise was big enough, consider these other, more relevant facts:

What are your long-range goals?

Do you like your job?

Do you like your company's long-term outlook?

Do you have a good opinion of your company's management?

What have you liked about your job since your last birthday? Did you progress in terms of responsibility? Or was the past year a boring period? How did you and your boss get along in the past year? If your relationship could have been better, what could you have done to contribute to this improvement? Is the rapport one-sided? Is it controlled exclusively by your boss?

Having a good rapport with your peers is also important to your progress with your company. Being a team player takes a lot of effort. On the one hand, you may be competing with your peers; on the other hand you try to do so on friendly terms. Generally speaking, there will be someone with whom you'll have difficulty, especially if, as an accountant, you have variable data that reflect on the performance of others. In particular, operating department managers may be on the defensive when your cost–budget variance letters or discussions bring out negative conclusions. How do you handle these situations diplomatically?

Your age and status will determine the self-improvement courses you can take or want to take. After all, the average accountant will have a 35- to 40-year career. Some self-improvement courses can be taken over and over again. We discussed Dale Carnegie and Toastmasters courses in an earlier chapter. Speed Reading, Effective Listening, Positive Thinking, Management Development are courses available in adult evening classes or college continuing education (noncredit) courses.

Most good presidents and general managers are profit-oriented and concerned with cost control. Most accountants are in an ideal position to initiate or suggest effective cost control procedures (internal auditing, variance analysis systems and procedure manuals, budgets) that can directly affect company profits. Your contributions in this area will determine your failure or success as an accountant. In his autobiography, Lee Iacocca had some fine things to say about accountants: "But as president my first concern was the relatively unglamorous task of searching out different ways to cut costs and increase profits. As a result, I was finally earning the respect of the one group that had always been suspicious of me—the bean counters" (Iacocca, 1984, p. 94). We accountants are the "bean counters."

☐ PLAN FOR YOUR NEXT BIRTHDAY

Now that you have reviewed last year's performance, you are ready to plan your next year.

Why bother to write out your plan? Can't you just remember it mentally for the next year? What's so important about putting it in writing?

You will be one of a select few if you plan your career in writing. By writing out your plan, you are committing yourself to your objectives, putting your credibility at stake. You are not to going to take the time and trouble to write out your goals for nothing. This has to be a serious plan, one that means a lot to your well-being and eventual self-image. By writing it out and then reviewing it a year later, you are giving yourself an incentive. You will find it exciting as you progress toward your objective.

Start off with your long-range goal, say five years, so that each year's plan will contain a slightly different and more advanced approach to that five-year goal.

Suppose you are 39 years old and you are manager of general accounting—what are your goals? To become division controller would be a reasonable goal. Take one goal at a time. To become corporation controller or president of the company probably is not a reasonable five-year goal.

Aim high, but use your judgment. Search out what you consider reasonably attainable goals, not long shots. Remember, when setting these goals, that you must face yourself if you don't attain your long-range goals. Make them flexible. At each birthday you can revise your five-year goal and also develop a new annual goal.

Remember that your career goals are not all you should think about on your birthday. Unless you also consider other goals in your life—financial, family, social, physical, and spiritual— your career goal development will become meaningless.

Exhibit 6.2 shows the résumé of "Ed Lucas," who was 39 years old in 1988 and was manager of general accounting for an $800 million corporation.

Exhibit 6.3 shows a five-year long-range projection (1988 through 1992) for Ed Lucas, including a promotion to assistant gear division controller in the next three years, and two years later to gear division controller. Remember, someone must make each decision to promote him. You should find out who will make that decision for your first planned promotion, and then guess who may be making it for your second position. Then begin concentrating on your five-year goal. One of Ed's plans is to become a CMA (certified management accountant). Another is membership in Toastmasters. Each educational objective is one that manage-

EXHIBIT 6.2. Résumé of Ed Lucas

Personal:	Age 39, 3 children, health excellent
Education:	BS Accounting, May 1971, University of Michigan. 3.2 GPA in Accounting, 3.6 GPA overall.
	CPA Certificate, state of Michigan, August, 1974. MBA Michigan State University, May 1975.
Position History:	Overland Motors, Gear Division, Detroit Michigan
7/76–present	Manager General Accounting: Supervise staff of 10 in $100 million division. Responsible for all accounting and analysis for 7 plants, including payables, receivables, credit, cash, payroll, consolidations, and financial statement preparation and analysis. Experienced with PC, IBM Systems 34 and 36, Lotus 1-2-3, and Symphony
9/71–6/76	Big Eight CPA Firm, Lansing, Michigan
	Supervise certified audits, staff of 4. Perform tax returns for smaller clients. Majority of clients are medium to large manufacturing and construction firms. Exposure to small and medium-sized, multistore retail firms
	Experienced in SEC (10K, 10Q), preparation for 2 clients.
Other:	Director of Membership, Oakland County Chapter, National Association of Accountants
	Treasurer, Northern Episcopal Church
	Member, MACPA, NACPA

ment would also consider a good move for the gear division and for the company as a whole. You must make your commitments at the appropriate time. Write down the specific week of the year in which you plan to apply to the CMA program. Find out the dates for the refresher course and the date the examinations are

EXHIBIT 6.3. Ed Lucas Career Planning as of June 15, 1987 (39th Birthday)

Age	Activity	Year(s)
39	Manager general accounting, gear division	1987
	Lotus 1-2-3 course	
42	Assistant controller, gear division	1988–1990
	CMA program (1988)	
	Dale Carnegie course (1989)	
	Join NAA (1990)	
45	Controller, gear division	1991–1992
	Join Toastmasters (1991)	
	Computer course (1992)	
50	Assistant transmission group controller	1993–1997
	Computer course (1993)	
51–55	Transmission group controller	1998–2002
56–65	Assistant corporate controller or assistant corporate treasurer or corporate director of accounting	2003–2013

given. Keep your superior apprised of your intentions and your attainments, as they occur. This is what I call low-key self-promotion. If you hope to succeed in a sophisticated environment, you must plan to use such self-promotion as you accomplish technical or educational objectives that are of value to the company.

Ed Lucas has three five-year plans and a ten-year plan spanning his entire work life. This may seem like too much for the average ambitious executive, but it's not at all ridiculous. You should have some idea of where and how you want your career to wind up. Your plan must read as though you have something to say about where you'd like to go. If you leave your career completely up to chance, you'll have no control over where it will probably end up.

During my 15 years in recruiting, I've met far too many technically qualified accountants who will nevertheless fail in their careers. The reasons are as follows:

They *don't* set specific goals.

They *don't* document specific goals.

They *don't* know how to set goals and review them.

They *don't* set goals because of the personal negative emotion they anticipate should they fail.

They *don't* have a good opinion of themselves; they lack self-esteem.

If they do have a good plan, its eventual execution was not good.

Since career planning is a lifelong process, it seems logical to begin this process when you enter college. In conjunction with counseling, your plans (such as they are) and college career planning courses, if available, should give you some idea of what you want to strive for in the next four years. Career planning is like a journey on which every step brings us to a different view. Each new view brings us closer to a better understanding of what our goals ought to be.

Any career-wise accountant who desires to maximize the greatest satisfaction from work needs a plan. The highest ranking executives in business are planners. Shouldn't you be a planner?

7

TO CHANGE OR NOT TO CHANGE—THAT IS THE QUESTION

I'm sure William Shakespeare would not mind my paraphrasing Hamlet's famous soliloquy to highlight a point. To change jobs or not to change jobs—that *is* the question. Your job is such an integral part of your total life that changing jobs is tantamount to starting a new life.

When you decide to change jobs, you actually have two very important decisions to make:

1. The decision to leave your present firm
2. The choice of another firm to work for

It's a lot like deciding to get divorced and then to remarry. Both choices can be traumatic or at least very difficult. In five job changes I experienced five different predominant emotions—happiness, sadness, fear, indecision, and panic. I also felt some shame, rage, and fatigue. If you are average, you also will make five job changes in your career, according to the American Management Association, and you will experience some of these emotions in the process—I guarantee it. But I hope that after reading this book and learning some new principles, you may prepare yourself to experience only sadness and happiness in your career moves— sadness at leaving your friends and co-workers at the old job, and happiness in your new job and new life. By wisely planning your career and job changes, you will tend to minimize fear, indecision, and panic. Yet the prospect of spending the rest of your career at a job where you are unhappy can influence you to begin making a decision to consider a job change.

Using your annual career planning day routinely for a review of your career can prepare you to make wiser decisions when the time comes to contemplate change. By anticipating career problems before they occur, you may be able to avoid career disasters.

☐ WHEN SHOULD YOU SERIOUSLY CONSIDER A JOB CHANGE?

It is almost impossible to predict accurately when you will decide to change employers. Sometimes you will have no choice in the matter, and your employers will have a great deal to say about whether you stay or go. Consideration for your families will be deeply involved in your decision-making process. The tumultuous changes in middle management in recent times have made true job security an elusive commodity.

Before you actually decide to plunge in and consider a job change, I suggest you first answer the following questions:

1. Are you convinced your career has reached an unacceptable plateau?
2. Are you experiencing burnout?
3. Are what you have accomplished and what you had hoped to accomplish miles apart?
4. Are you emotionally able to handle a job change?
5. How hard did you take it when you lost out on a promotion?
6. Will you be happy elsewhere?
7. Are you deathly afraid of your next appraisal?
8. Are your peers also unhappy in their jobs?
9. Do you discuss your job and profession negatively with anyone who will listen?

10. Do you live exclusively for your weekends?

11. Do you daydream about being in another profession?

1. *Are you convinced your career has reached an unacceptable plateau?* If, as discussed in Chapter 5, you have reviewed your situation thoroughly, and your job is at an unacceptable standstill, you should consider a job change—that is, if you are not in middle management, you are not over 50, and your city or state is not in an economic recession or depression.

Remember that at this point you have only made a decision that a job change is in order. You are a long way from having a new job or making arrangements for a severance.

2. *Are you experiencing burnout?* A CFO earning $100,000 once called me and literally begged me to find him an easier, less demanding job. The pressure and responsibility this CFO was experiencing were so overwhelming to him that he was willing to take a 50 percent cut in pay to find peace of mind. But when I finally saw this man face to face, in the winter of 1979, I was convinced he was not suffering from job burnout—he was literally suffering from overwork. He had been working 60 hours a week for two years without a vacation. I suggested he take a vacation from his job. He came back from Fort Meyers, Florida, tanned, refreshed, and eager to tackle any new problem. From that day on, that CFO made it a habit to take several vacations each year. I have not heard from him since. I lost an applicant—but he was not ready to change jobs despite his panicky condition at that moment.

If you think you are suffering a job burnout, perhaps a vacation or leave of absence may be in order. If you are still depressed and out of control when you return, you may need the services of a psychologist or even a psychiatrist before throwing in the towel.

3. *Are what you have accomplished and what you had hoped to accomplish miles apart?* First consider whether you have had or been given the right tools to accomplish your goals. Who or what prevented you from succeeding? Did you yourself foul up? Could someone else have succeeded where you didn't? Analyze these questions carefully. Looking back, were your goals reasonable? Maybe your estimate of how long it would take, for example, to be promoted to controller, was overoptimistic. Perhaps the

controller himself was not promoted or did not leave voluntarily. You had no control over this situation; there simply was no opening for you to be promoted. Are you reasonably sure you would be a candidate for that position if the controller did leave in the near future? Are you willing to wait to find out—or are you ready to move on now? It might not be a bad idea to ask your supervisors if you would be in the running for the position should there be an opening. Then you can react to their answer.

4. *Are you emotionally able to handle a job change?* One of the most important considerations is whether you can handle a job change. Are you confident that your technical abilities and interviewing techniques, and the job market, will carry you through to a new and better position?

It is difficult to predict how long it will take you to find a better job, from the time you decide to begin job hunting. Once you have made that decision, it will be very difficult for you to maintain a high level of effort, energy, and enthusiasm. You may tip off your employer that in fact you are putting more concentration into other areas of interest. You will be taking the risk that your boss may sense that something is not right, and may even call you in and ask you about your intentions. Many of my applicants have told me they were asked directly: "Are you looking for a new job?"

By observing your facial expressions, an experienced boss can usually tell if you are lying or not, especially if you are basically an honest person. Of the five times I changed jobs, only twice was I in a position where my boss did not know I was looking for greener pastures, and could not detect my intentions. Fortunately, in both cases, I seldom came in close contact with my supervisor, because each had a large staff.

One young applicant came to see me regarding his intention of changing jobs for the first time in his short career. Not only was he drenched in sweat when he sat down, but he also began to stutter badly, although he had no history of stuttering. He could not continue the interview. That was such a shock for him that he decided not to pursue a new job. Instead of calling me, he sent me a note indicating that he would rather maintain his unhappy status quo than confront the challenges of a job change.

In the fall of 1987 I retrieved this young man's records out of our company's inactive file on the assumption that he was still with the same employer. Five years had passed since I had last talked with him. After I asked him about his interest in making a change, he said, with clear diction and no stuttering, "I'm happy where I am." He had become an assistant controller three years ago, and, surprisingly, there were no signs of a single stutter during our two-minute phone conversation.

When I asked him about his stuttering, he replied that he still stutters, but only in extremely stressful situations. I concluded that he had never really solved his problem, although he is keeping it under control. The problem of a lack of promotion possibilities still persists, although he did attain the rank of assistant controller. Perhaps that will be his peak performance.

Another applicant, a retail treasurer, called me to announce that he wanted to meet me for a confidential interview. He would identify himself only as Mr. A. After several calls to pick a date and time, when Mr. A finally showed up, he proceeded to look under the table for a tape recorder, despite my assurances that the room was not bugged. It wasn't until our interview was finished that he decided to reveal his name and release his résumé to me.

5. *How hard did you take it when you lost out on a promotion?* This is a hard blow to take, particularly if you thought you were the most qualified applicant and were anticipating it. Do a thorough analytical review of the candidate who did get the job. This may take time. Try to compare his qualifications to yours, objectively. Review his experience, education, personality, and politics, and honestly compare them to yours.

If the results show that your competitor was more qualified, so be it. Stop feeling bad, and move on. But before you do, try to find out what you could have done better, or where you fell short, compared to your competitor. If it is your lack of an MBA that's the problem, that may be possible to alter. If it's a CPA certificate that you lack, that may be more difficult to overcome. If your personality needs to become more aggressive, there may be things you can do to overcome this shortcoming.

6. *Will you be happy elsewhere?* Be sure that is true before you leap. The grass always seems greener on the other side, but is it really? You must find the root cause of your unhappiness. If you are married and have a family, are you unhappy at home? Are

you unhappy as a single or divorced person? In the course of an interview, I generally ask about the candidate's home life and family health. I'm never amazed to hear that a divorce is imminent while, at the same time, the candidate's job is in jeopardy. In most cases, home life situations and office happiness are intertwined. It's possible that once you solve your home life problems, your job attitude will also improve. And, once your job situation improves, the quality of your home life often will seem to improve as well.

7. *Are you deathly afraid of your next appraisal?* My annual appraisals, with companies with over $1 billion in sales, were difficult for me because I had ten new bosses in nine years with the same company. (Smaller companies did not use formal appraisals.) I never knew what to expect in the appraisal. One supervisor was very severe in his criticism of my activities, even though throughout the year we had not appeared to have any problems worth mentioning. Another supervisor gave me glowing superlatives, even though his assignments were generally simple, not very challenging and not requiring any significant talent. However, I always felt a little tense before and during the appraisal session. If you foresee disaster in your next appraisal, you may very well contemplate an exit or transfer in the near future, preferably before the appraisal goes on your official record. It would be a good idea to know *why* you foresee a disastrous appraisal. Was it your doing? Could it have been avoided? If you constantly resort to rationalization and use excuses for your actions, it will be very difficult for you to use good judgment in concluding that a change is in order. You must be completely honest with yourself, about yourself and about the consequences of your actions.

8. *Are your peers also unhappy?* If you, as cost accounting manager, are having difficulty with what you consider to be a merciless boss, and no one else has the same opinion, you may have a serious career problem. Obviously, if all the other managers reporting to this same boss are cringing, too, for the same reasons, then you know it may not just be you. It could be the boss who is unreasonable.

The question is: What plan of action can you make? Quitting or changing jobs should always be considered only as a last resort. Otherwise you would be changing jobs every time you were unhappy, and soon you would have no career.

"William Geiser," age 45, dropped into my office unannounced one morning. His résumé showed he had been with a small distributor firm as an accountant for 18 years. He sadly explained that the reason he wanted to change jobs was that his boss was "mean." Further clarification revealed that his boss passed him in the halls "without even saying hello" or acknowledging him. He seemed devastated. Other than that, he liked his job. He said that the boss treated other employees in the same manner.

My advice to Mr. Geiser was not to take it personally. The boss probably had other things on his mind and was not aware of his actions. I suggested he rethink his decision to change jobs, and I believe he took my advice, as he did not return. Our follow-up revealed he was still with the firm two years later, although the situation had not changed. He adapted to it, and is now happy on the job. His reasons for a job change were not valid.

9. *Do you discuss your job and profession negatively with anyone who will listen?* When you are unhappy with your job, there is a tendency to reflect this unhappiness. Some candidates will tell everyone within shouting distance about their terrible job, the problems it is causing, and how unfair it is.

I never complained to my peers or friends at the office. I considered any dissatisfaction with my bosses or jobs my personal, private problem. I discussed my situation only with my wife and my closest friends.

Business maturity dictates that as long as you are working with or for human beings, you will have social and relationship problems. You will never escape them. A roll-with-the-punches attitude is a good one to have. Not everyone is happy at the same time. All the people we deal with have moods that change from day to day. We must accept this as a fact of life on the job and not get caught up in accepting the moods of others as our own.

Revealing your innermost feelings at the office for all to hear does not make good business sense, since this confidential information may find itself on the office gossip grapevine and eventually reach the ears of management. Keep complaints to yourself during work hours. Complain if you must, as a release, but only to your trusted friends. If you have what you feel is a legitimate complaint that can affect your physical or mental health, speak to someone at the proper level of the hierarchy—and do it tactfully.

Willingness to tell everyone about your job unhappiness is a career death wish. You probably should consider a new position if you have reached that point. But make sure you are not jumping from the proverbial frying pan into the fire.

10. *Do you live for your weekends exclusively?* This is a red flag, an indication that something is wrong with your job and perhaps with your career. A fifty-fifty appreciation of office life and home life would be ideal. However, those figures will change to 80-20, 70-30, 30-70, and so on, in the short run, and still be close to 50-50 in the long haul. I could write a book on "How to Love Your Job," but in this case your objective is to love both your job and your home life at the same time. It *is* possible. As a certified personnel consultant, however, I can only counsel you on your job and your career in this book.

From a career-planning standpoint, living for your weekends exclusively seems to indicate that your five work days lack high-quality living and could be a horrible waste of your own and your company's time. If you were putting your full effort and concentration into your job, and were producing to the best of your ability, then you would not be living exclusively for your weekends. Living fully only two out of seven days indicates that serious job attitude problems loom on the horizon. It would be prudent to take action before the problem becomes so overwhelming that you will not be able to cope with it—for example, when all your peers are being promoted while you still live only for your weekends. Again, this is a red flag that will pop up when you make your annual career plan.

Take time to analyze why you are living for your weekends exclusively. You must understand the situation and develop a plan to change. It's possible a job change is in order if your self-analysis brings you to that conclusion. Again, before deciding to change jobs, you first want to consider changes you can make internally.

11. *Do you daydream about being in another profession?* Most accountants will not admit to daydreaming. They prefer to say

they *think* about another position. The psychologists also seem to shy away from the word *daydream* and have developed a new one—*visualization*. I also prefer this term. I think it attempts to avoid the negative connotations associated with daydreaming.

If we follow through with action, I believe, we can become what we visualize. However, an overindulgence in thinking about another profession is an easy symptom to diagnose. You are probably sick of your present situation and longing for a change. If you have already exhausted all means at your disposal to cope with your present position, then you should take your "daydreams" seriously—if they are realistic (e.g., becoming a consultant, entrepreneur, or financial planner).

Dreams such as moving to Tahiti as a CFO may have to be disregarded, although some psychologists say that such daydreams can help relieve pressure and tensions at the proper time. So keep on daydreaming.

☐ HOW TO RESIGN WITH CLASS

"Mr. Browning, I have accepted a new position with another corporation, as financial analyst. I am giving you my two weeks notice. I enjoyed my three years with X Corporation; however, my new company's salary and opportunities for my career needs were outstanding. I could not refuse their offer. Thanks for everything."

These are approximately the words I used to the assistant corporate controller when I resigned my cost accounting position. Needless to say, there was a counteroffer, which I promptly rejected. That was very early in my accounting career. I left with a blessing and good wishes from Mr. Browning, who understood.

My reasons for declining the counteroffer were as follows:

1. The fact that I resigned indicated to management that my loyalty to the company was questionable. That would probably be a factor in the future, especially if I were in the running for a key promotion, where loyalty, among other considerations, was to be reviewed.

2. From my standpoint, I would always wonder: Will I have to threaten to resign to get my next raise? Since I was an accountant with a low classification, I doubted that the company would change their policy on my account.

3. This counteroffer strategy indicated that the company had a weakness in salary reviews as well as in routine management reviews. The company I was to start with had a more sophisticated approach to annual reviews, and the salary structure was published in a small booklet passed on to all new employees in the accounting department.

4. The fact that my salary increase was so high and the company was still willing to match it indicated that they knew I was grossly underpaid, but were willing to overlook this situation. Management should review salaries of employees routinely.

Not all bosses take a resignation from their employees that favorably or without some trepidation. In my early years as a manager, I unrealistically viewed a resignation of my employees as a "divorce"—a personal failure on my part. As I matured and studied these resignations more closely, I realized that in the main it was for the best. There were exceptions, where I succeeded in changing a valued employee's mind. In this case, only salary was a problem and I corrected that—not by a counteroffer, which I do not believe in, but with future salary increases tacked on to goal achievements.

Telling a boss off and burning all your bridges must be frowned on and considered poor judgment that could easily boomerang. Play it cool and use dignity in your final dealing with your former employers. You must think in terms of future references, your exit interview with your personnel department, and your career reputation as a whole.

If there was bad blood between you and your boss, and your boss goads you into telling him the real reason you are leaving, you must use your will power not to turn your resignation into a verbal shouting match and another confrontation.

Exiting with dignity is advisable, since sometime in the future you may need the blessing of your former employer. It would be a good idea to ask for and obtain a written letter of reference before you leave. This way, if your letter of reference is not complimentary, you may have a chance to get an explanation or even a rewrite. I have yet to see a bad letter of reference. Companies' legal departments frown on company representatives giving out damaging references, because of possible lawsuits.

Treat your resignation and exit review on the same level as if you were interviewing for a new job. Put your best foot forward, doing everything possible to leave with a positive, professional image. This is a part of your career planning that is not taught in curriculums in colleges today.

What to Do When You Lose Your Job Involuntarily

Outplacement. If your company does not offer you the services of an outplacement firm, you should request it in your release negotiation package. More and more firms throughout the United States are engaging these services to insulate themselves against possible lawsuits by disgruntled fired employees.

Involuntary job loss could result from poor performance, reorganization, bankruptcy, acquisition, mental incompetency, or another cause. If you are being released, you want to find out why, and the outplacement firm will tell you. Many times the outplacement firm actually performs the firing, without the boss's presence, because of a fear that the released employee will become violent upon seeing the boss who made the decision.

Outplacement is an organized plan to help terminated employees find a new path of employment, while reducing the emotional shock associated with losing a job. The benefits to the employee are as follows:

1. It diminishes stress by the use of trained counseling.
2. You can ascertain your positive and marketable qualities and assess your career potential.
3. It provides preparation by developing the best and most marketable résumé and associated letters.
4. It provides private office and telephone support, even after five to six weeks of counseling.

5. It provides inspirational pamphlets for other members of your family to help them support you.

Most outplacement firms offer career testing and evaluation as part of their services to the outplacee. Our firm's studies show that over 90 percent of terminated employees remain in the same field. Therefore, we feel a lot of time and expense is wasted on this testing. We believe that career testing should be made only in exceptional and isolated cases, and only if the previous boss deems it necessary. Most terminated employees are severed from their positions because of personality conflicts, philosophy conflicts, and temporary mood excesses, not necessarily because they chose the wrong profession. A small percentage of accountants find that, in fact, they have chosen the wrong profession. Only one CPA out of 500 that I interviewed was convinced he was in the wrong field, though I did not agree with him; his conclusion was influenced by his boss's opinion.

Some accountants have used their accounting education and experience to prepare them for fields such as consulting, recruiting, teaching, tax law, financial planning, and banking, to name a few.

The company that offers outplacement services benefits in the following manner:

1. There is less anger and resentment associated with the termination process.
2. It improves goodwill for fellow employees who were not terminated.
3. It minimizes the possibility of a lawsuit by an unhappy employee.
4. The outplacee is exposed to positive attitude techniques that give him a better chance to find a new job.
5. Reductions in middle management are on the upswing nationwide. Outplacement is a natural system for termination and staff reductions.
6. Outplacement helps a company maintain a favorable corporate self-image in the eyes of the local community.

Networking

You have probably heard about networking, but unless you are unemployed you may not have had too much opportunity to use it to the fullest. If you have many years of experience and have accumulated a sizable list of acquaintances who are capable of hiring accountants, then you already have a network ready to operate.

The executive who is good at maintaining a network list is, in effect, using career game-planning techniques. Networking offers one of the few advantages older accountants have over younger ones—the contacts they have made over the years should pay dividends.

My observations suggest that many more accountants land jobs in this way than through traditional means. But don't make the mistake of using the "buddy network" exclusively. This technique is only one of many an unemployed accountant must use if he wants the right position as soon as possible.

The first step is to have one executive introduce your name to another, so that your network keeps expanding, pyramid fashion. Setting a goal of five new contacts a day is ideal. These are people who may have heard of job openings or can give you names of someone else to call. It would be a tactical mistake to be too proud to ask for assistance from your business acquaintances. You will be surprised how quickly many buddies will be willing to help you if you are in need. Outplacement firms strongly counsel terminated employees to use networking extensively. Of the five job changes I have made, networking with professional association members (NAA) resulted in my obtaining two controller positions. Two other times I found jobs directly by answering Help Wanted ads in the local Sunday newspaper. The fifth job I obtained by sending an unsolicited résumé directly to the personnel department of a large company where I had always wanted to work.

Begin attending every meeting of the professional associations you belong to, and attend meetings as a guest where you do not have an active membership. Don't curtail all your association costs and memberships just to save money. Treat all your association expenses as potential investments in acquiring a new job and maintaining or advancing in your career goal. The more meetings you attend, the more your network will grow and the better your chances are of accelerating your job search.

Overextend yourself at association meetings. Go around shaking hands and introducing yourself as if you were running for governor. Have special calling cards printed and distribute them to anyone who will accept one. During the question/answer period at association meetings, be sure to get up and ask relevant and well-thought-out-questions. Make sure you enunciate your name loudly and clearly for all in attendance to hear. At an NAA meeting I asked a question, then clearly stated, "My name is Henry Labus, and I'm presently seeking a new position." I had several potential employers seek me out after the meeting. If you plan right, the associations can be an excellent place for you to operate your networking strategy. Place an ad in your professional association newsletter.

If you are over 40, you might join the nonprofit Forty Plus Club in your area. A typical club has typewriters available for updating résumés. It's something like Alcoholics Anonymous in that prospective members are introduced to other members and have a chance to explain the chain of events that led to losing their job. Members offer peer support and fresh ideas for job searches. They even ring a bell and make an announcement when a member accepts a new position. As of 1985 the initiation cost was $300, with an additional $300 exit fee when a member finds a position. There is a minimal weekly housekeeping expense. Forty Plus offers a unique résumé service and interview courses in which a job counseling committee spends a great deal of time and effort in perfecting résumés that get results. The Club also receives notice of openings from corporations, and the committee tries to match applicants with job opportunities.

Recruiters

Executive recruiting firms generally find jobs for highly marketable, well-qualified, personable candidates—the cream of the crop. Their loyalty rests principally with the employer, because employers are the ones that compensate these firms for their services. So don't be too concerned if an agency does not cater to you immediately. They will when they find a match.

There is a fine distinction between employment agencies and recruiting (search) firms. Both attempt to fill positions with the best candidates available for the job, according to rigid specifications. Search firms may be paid for services rendered (whether they fill the job or not) plus reimbursement of applicable travel and phone expenses. Employment agencies generally operate on a contingency basis: They do not get paid unless the company hires their recommended candidate. If the agency fails to recruit the right candidate, there is no fee to the company. There are many excellent search firms and employment agencies that specialize in recruiting accountants. One employment agency in Chicago specializes exclusively in tax specialists. Another, in Florida, recruits only CPAs. There are also some fine employment agencies that service all professions, including accounting. Our firm specializes in finance and attorneys, and we are staffed with seasoned attorneys and accountants.

As an unemployed accountant, you should first seek out a few reputable firms specializing in your field. You will find that well-educated CPAs, MBAs, or CPCs (certified personnel consultants) may be assisting you through this difficult period. But remember that employment agencies obtain only 10 percent of all the available openings at any given time. Our breakdown of available accounting job openings is as follows:

Unadvertised by company	40%
Help Wanted ads	25%
Employment agencies/search firms	10%
Other	10%
College placement services	5%
CPA firms	10%
	100%

Who pays the fee? As an applicant, you don't, if you are dealing with a reputable agency or search firm. Gone are the days when professionals themselves were asked to pay fees. Even though you may be unemployed, resist the temptation to send your résumé to all the agencies and recruiters listed in the Yellow Pages. Client companies' personnel departments do not appreciate getting the same résumé from four or five different agencies. Limit your recruiters to three of the best and most reputable. Insist on dealing with a recruiter who has been an accountant, preferably a former financial executive. It's no different than insisting on having a heart specialist treat you for a heart condition.

Temporary Positions

If you're unemployed, should you accept a temporary position while earnestly looking for a permanent one? Absolutely. An active, busy accountant is more apt to stay enthusiastic and be better prepared when the time comes to interview for a permanent job. Nowadays, employment agencies have fine temporary openings for general accountants, cost accountants, tax specialists, managers, and controllers. The added income will help sustain you financially and boost your self-esteem. Waiting in the unemployment line does little to bolster an accountant's confidence and pride. There may also be another by-product of taking a temporary job. Some companies hire temporary employees for permanent positions as an excellent way of testing and observing accountants with the objective of hiring them if they're good. Since temporary assignments usually last a few months at most, you may have an opportunity to work for a number of companies before you find a permanent position. Good companies always look for good people; if you impress them as a temp, it could lead to a permanent job. Temporary work also offers you an opportunity to evaluate a company before actually accepting a permanent position if it is offered—not a bad way to have your cake and eat it, too.

In 1987 "Harry Tovaris," a tax specialist from a medium-sized Southfield CPA firm, lost his job when his company learned that he was actively seeking a new position. Our company had recently entered the temporary field, specializing in accounting positions. The director of taxes at American Motors had advised me he would consider hiring a temporary tax specialist, with the idea of hiring permanently if the candidate worked out. The match was perfect. The candidate was interested in such an arrangement even though he was capable of obtaining per diem work on his own at a much higher hourly salary.

More and more companies are using this method of locating talented accountants. Normally, two months is long enough to determine if there is a match.

☐ MIDLIFE CRISES (CHANGES IN LIFE)

Why bring up midlife crises at all? Shouldn't we sweep this term under the rug as we have been doing for the past few decades? Absolutely not!

Midlife crises affect all of us at one time or another. We should be able to recognize their signs in ourselves and in those working with or around us. We will become better managers if we learn to use to advantage the knowledge that approaching middle age and feelings of mortality are normal facts of life, and that life is not passing us by as we may feel at times.

Webster's New Collegiate Dictionary (1981) describes *middle age* as "the period of life from about 40 to about 60." Your boss or your associates may very well be in this age bracket, though most 40-year-olds would deny that they have reached "middle age" so soon. Middle age, I think, comes when you've met so many people that every new person reminds you of someone else. In the past 20 years, middle age has become more of a psychological phenomenon than a physical one. You just don't feel young any more—and the majority of people I interviewed indicate they have no desire to be young again.

You age a little every day without really noticing it—a few more gray hairs, wrinkles, changes in your jawline in the mirror. The inevitable movement of age, coupled with the stresses of living, begins to make you more susceptible to illness than you were. Your doctors tell you to stop smoking, give up coffee, and so on. You feel that time is speeding up, and you may begin to brood over your "wasted" years. Other symptoms include insecurity, depression, indecisiveness, a feeling of impending disaster, a feeling that time has passed you by, nervousness, restlessness, a feeling of being trapped, and an obsession with old age and death. Have you recently noticed that your co-worker, "Old Ed," seems inconsistent, bitter, resentful, defensive, and very different in emotion and attitude than he used to be? Good accounting managers should learn to recognize the reality of someone else's midlife crisis as well as their own. It's good business sense. As manager, you should work with Ed and others like him. Attempt to make Ed feel he is entering an age of opportunity, not approaching a dead end. Give him real assignments, not busy work. Ed needs to keep his self-respect as an employee. He has accumulated many years of knowledge and wisdom that can be tapped. Knowingly allowing an employee to vegetate is unthinkable; it is too costly to the company. Although what your fellow employees make of middle age is their own responsibility, it doesn't hurt to help them along.

We're at a peak risk of experiencing our first major depression between the ages of 45 and 55. Ten men and 15 women per 1,000 will experience such a depression. In middle age most of us begin to be exposed to major setbacks—the loss of our own parents, career problems, and the like—and we don't have such strong buffers anymore. Depression is a road no middle-aged person should have to travel alone.

Can you plan for middle age? Of course. If you use your annual career day plan religiously, you should plan not to fall into this rut. Then you'll be able to recognize the symptoms and make the proper personal adjustments. These adjustments can become part of your annual career planning day objectives.

How do I handle middle age? So far, it's been the most thrilling and rewarding part of my life. Although I do recognize the numbers representing my age, I don't see them as a disadvantage, but as a challenge and an opportunity. I have made plenty of foolish mistakes in managing my own career, but I have survived. Perhaps some accountants who have not made those same mistakes can profit from my knowledge. Of course, it's better for you and your career *not* to make mistakes. Many times, however, it's just a lack of knowledge or concentration that causes them.

Norm Henning, my loyal, silver-haired assistant, is a fine example of a person who has planned specific stages of his midlife successfully. He's now 67 and is enjoying every minute of his life. He skipped the midlife crises that most people go through. At age 55 Norm left a controller's position to join our firm as his second career. His transition was excellent. At age 60 he studied hard and became a certified personnel consultant. At 67, Norm still does consulting work for our firm. All along, he has been involved with his church and has traveled extensively with his wife of 36 years. Norm *planned* his golden years, and he has executed his plan well.

Changing Careers in Midlife

Succeeding in a second career in midlife can be difficult. Yet, if you are successful, it can really be satisfying.

What do you do to develop a second career?

1. If dissatisfied with your present job, look at yourself in the mirror and ask yourself what you want.
2. If you have lost your job, get control of yourself.
3. Learn the art of selling yourself in the accountant's market.
4. Allow yourself four to six months, maybe more, to get off the floor, to attain your objective.
5. Don't allow pessimists to discourage you because of your age—treat it as a powerful tool.
6. Don't do it alone. Your family or close friends should be at your side, helping you make the right decisions.

☐ WHAT TO DO WHEN YOUR COMPANY IS ACQUIRED

Mergers and acquisitions have been a fact of corporate life for a long time, but their frequency has accelerated in the past five years. Suppose you hear through the grapevine that your company is about to be acquired by a larger firm. None of your college textbooks covers career planning during an acquisition. If there's a chapter on consolidations, it won't help. Your boss is probably in the same boat you are.

What do you do?

1. Punt?
2. Bring your dusty résumé up to date?

3. Keep calm?
4. Do nothing?
5. Look for a power struggle?
6. Consider what you would do if you were demoted?
7. Consider being promoted?

I would say you do all seven things at different stages of the acquisition.

During the acquisition negotiations process, most managers feel apprehensive about their future with the new company, even though they normally hear that "There's nothing to worry about, the staff will be kept intact." It's when you hear that that you should begin to be seriously concerned. Even if the headline in the local newspapers states "No Changes Expected," don't believe it. One of the objects of a merger and acquisition is to get the most efficient use of people, meaning to have fewer people do more work, faster and more accurately.

There's no doubt that if you are a tax specialist, cash manager, or internal auditor, your job may be in jeopardy. This is usually a corporate function. If your record is outstanding, the chances are you may have a job, but at another location. Are you prepared?

Division controllers will be in a risky situation, since it's relatively simple to make, say, two divisions out of three. If you have played the game of office politics effectively, you may have accumulated many points with your superior, who will try to do the best for you. But if you haven't played politics, or if you know your performance has been only "acceptable," you may be wise to make preparations for departure. In evaluating your situation, be honest with yourself. Rationalization will not help.

When you hear serious rumors about the pending acquisition, begin protecting your job. (Realistically, you should have been doing this right along.) The idea is to put your job in a holding pattern until you decide exactly where you are and what you are going to do about it.

I have thought of five things you can do to protect your job:

1. Review details of your duties and responsibilities, and be prepared to explain them to your new superior. Review

your personal accomplishments and put them in writing.

2. Review, comprehend, and be able to explain accurately the function of each of your staff members. Do this in writing, also, if you want to keep your staff.

3. Look to the new corporate decision makers for overall policy pronouncements, and ask where you and your department fit in.

4. Appear calm and collected. Be patient with disruptions in routine and discussion of new policies and procedures. Your new bosses will observe how you handle yourself during this stressful period. This is not the time to panic.

5. Remain neutral in any upper management power struggle that looms on the horizon. If you are forced to choose, be sure to give your decision plenty of serious thought. Try not to make your choice on the basis of emotion or friendship— it may cost you your job.

During negotiations, accept the fact that you will *not* be kept fully informed. No matter what you are told, anything can happen when the new bosses begin functioning. Unless you have promises in writing, expect the unexpected. Then punt.

Take the case of a large Texas firm that acquired a smaller, though sizable firm. During negotiations, the president assured the smaller firm's employees that there would be no changes in personnel or policy. Within a week I had résumés of all the top executives in the tax department on file. The new firm offered the director of taxes an assistant director's position in Texas with no loss in pay, but after several trips to Texas during the summer he declined the transfer and eventually found an acceptable job locally. Most of the tax department staff people likewise began looking for new positions. In fact, a year or so later, so many people had left that the department was understaffed, and the company had to recruit new tax people—at higher salaries.

There may even be some positive factors during an acquisition:

1. You may be better qualified than any other candidates for your job or for a higher job for which you have the requisite talents.

2. The new company may not be as familiar with your company's product line as you are. They may need you to teach them the finer points of the business or the department.

3. Generally speaking, bigger companies offer better fringe benefits than smaller ones do. They may also have higher salary scales and more liberal educational policies.

4. Termination pay could be lucrative. Negotiate a shrewd package if you can. I know of a manager who negotiated a year's pay termination while he proceeded to find a job within one month.

As a manager, you may be facing other problems, including maintaining the loyalty of those reporting to you and attempting to assure them that their jobs are not in jeopardy.

1. You may be unsure of your own position.

2. Salaries may be frozen for an unspecified period, until they are evaluated.

3. There will be unfamiliar new people roaming about the office and wanting to know who does what, when, and where.

4. Your assistants may have heard gossip about how entire sections and departments of other firms have been eliminated.

5. Communication is probably at its lowest ebb, since the ashes have not yet been sifted. You should, however, be honest in telling your staff quickly any new information you have that could affect them.

Older employees, even marginal ones, who are between 55 and 60 and who have years of seniority, probably will not be the first to go in an acquisition. Companies are too frightened by the possibility of being sued for age discrimination. Also, they may prefer to keep mature employees until retirement and try to get the most out of them. Older employees have a lot to offer the company—their experience and acquired skills.

8

CAREER CHANGES

Typically, accountants are college graduates who have majored in accounting or finance. We accountants tend to envision ourselves as succeeding in our field. With a silver lance held high in one hand and a diploma in the other, we charge full speed into the sunset, seeking adventure, riches, and success.

Then what happens? We come to a fork in the road—and there are no road signs. We take out our map, our dream of success. That map showed us the avenues to success, but it did not show us the obstacles or roadblocks we would encounter. No one in college warned us about these roadblocks—our competitors, our shortcomings, our poor work habits, our lack of drive, and so forth.

Unmarked forks in the road will pop up at many important points in your career. You will wonder, then, about the logic of making a career change. This will occur, most likely, when you are discouraged or fed up with your present position or circumstance, such as when

you have just lost your job.

you have just been demoted.

you didn't get an anticipated raise.

you and your boss are having serious difficulties.

you are entering midlife.

you are having marital problems.

I would guess that about one in three of our applicants who have lost their jobs ask us about changing careers. They have experienced a setback, and they believe their career let them down, so they inquire about a new career. They don't necessarily proceed in that direction. I usually suggest that they first attempt to find an accounting position. If in six months they still feel the same way, then I will try to advise them on how to proceed with a career change.

Changing careers isn't difficult. But changing to the *right* career, and succeeding at it, is no easy task. Fifty percent of those starting new businesses fail in the first year, a staggering 90 percent within eight years. Changing careers can mean going into business for yourself (a fast food franchise, your own CPA office, employment counseling), or becoming a salesperson, a marketing specialist, or a consultant.

In contemplating any change at all, I suggest you first go through a written evaluation of yourself. Answer the following questions:

1. What are your talents and special skills?
2. What are five of your achievements and successes in your vocation or avocation?
3. What are three things you now enjoy doing and are good at?
4. Given the chance, what would you like to do for the balance of your career?
5. Are you willing to take the risk of failing? Can you handle failure emotionally?
6. Financially, can you afford to make the change? You must expect to have a smaller income at first, until you get off the ground.

Once you know what your strongest talents are, you can seek the field that best fits your skills. If you have many talents, it may be more difficult to zero in on the *one* best talent or interest.

If you are a risk-averse individual, willing to do almost anything to avoid the possibility of an uncomfortable situation cropping up in your daily life or on the job, then changing careers could become a disaster for you.

As you analyze yourself and wrestle with the thought of a career change, ask yourself: Why am I looking for or considering a career change? Are my expectations realistic? Am I going through a personality conflict with the boss or close associates? Have I been thinking about changing courses for a long time, or is this a recent whim? This chapter offers a review of entrepreneurship, sales or marketing, consulting, and public accounting as possible alternatives to your present position.

☐ ENTREPRENEURSHIP

A person who organizes and manages a business undertaking, assuming the risk involved for the sake of a potential profit, is called an *entrepreneur*. I have been engaged in entrepreneurship for the past 16 years as my second career. My first career, accounting, lasted 20 years, in which I moved up the ladder from junior accountant; through cost accountant, price, budget, and financial analyst; to plant, division, and finally corporate controller. Although I *liked* my accounting career, I *love* being an entrepreneur.

How did I manage to change careers? Sixteen years ago my controller's position was eliminated because of an acquisition. My period of mourning lasted just one weekend, as I experienced the sorrow and humiliation of being rejected by a corporation. I liked my job and wasn't happy about leaving it. The next Monday, I visited a reputable employment agency specializing in accounting. After a brief interview, the owner-manager asked me if I was interested in making a career change into recruiting.

I was not yet ready to leave the accounting profession. But I was offered a temporary position as an accounting recruiter while I waited for interviews to materialize for a permanent controller's position. Evidently this manager saw potential character traits in me that I myself didn't see. He himself had changed careers; he was a registered engineer turned accounting recruiter, who had purchased this employment agency franchise after finishing his MBA.

The agency owner turned out to be a genius. How did he know that within two months I would completely fall in love with my new career? What tipped the scale for me was the good feeling I had about finding jobs for accountants. It was a satisfying, almost spiritual feeling. Not only that—I was also getting paid for doing something I enjoyed.

For two years, I felt like a priest or a psychologist as I listened to my applicants' problems and then attempted to solve them. If I didn't actually find them a job, I could at least advise them on how to find a new and perhaps better one. Sometimes I even recommended that applicants stay with their present firm. In the midst of the 1971 recession, I decided to become an entrepreneur and founded my own recruiting firm.

How did other American entrepreneurs acquire their businesses? According to a survey by the prominent Laventhol & Harvath (CPA) firm, 42 percent started from scratch, 23 percent purchased an existing business, 22 percent took over a family business, 5 percent started as a spinoff from a larger company, while the remaining 8 percent gave another response or didn't know the answer. Entrepreneuring is definitely making a comeback in the United States. Bob McCracken, our company's CPA, who is one of the most knowledgeable and talented CPAs in Michigan, asked me what were the most important traits needed to become a successful entrepreneur. This was my response:

Enjoyment of hard work and accomplishment
Persistence
Patience
Self-confidence
Financial backing
A broad general knowledge of how a business operates

Enjoyment of Hard Work and Accomplishment

Being an entrepreneur isn't for everyone. The roots of entrepreneurship begin developing early in life. My first responsible job was as a newsboy for the Niagara Falls *Gazette*. Jobs followed as pin-setter in a bowling alley, produce clerk in a grocery store, caddy at a country club, and janitor at a university while I worked my way through college. Each job required hard work, and the income helped my family and myself through lean years.

Most entrepreneurs work harder than the people they hire as they begin to grow. Although I worked many hours to get my company started, in the 16 years we've been in business, I've never asked my employees to work overtime or on weekends. Instead, I try to get them to give their maximum productivity during regular work hours.

Being your own boss is one of the great American dreams. Where else can you wear so many different hats—boss, salesman, accountant, secretary, and so on?

Persistence

This is one character trait that I believe is absolutely the most important. If you don't have it or don't develop it, your chances of survival in a highly competitive field are almost nil—and I don't know of any fields that are *not* fiercely competitive. Most businesses have cycles, which are not always predictable. When orders and sales are down, you have to dig in and persevere. When cash flow is low, you tighten your belt. You can't be discouraged when one of your top employees leaves your firm. You can't throw in the towel when two major newspapers go on strike even though you depend on newspapers to draw business.

During recessions (which are frequent in Michigan because of the nature of the auto industry), you just work harder and, again, tighten your belt, even while the world around you goes into a panic. With positive thinking on your side, you just know that better times are coming—and they usually do.

You must be brave enough to try new ideas, products, services, and markets, though you don't know whether they will succeed or even get you off the ground. I still remember the thrill of proudly opening the office door on my first day at work, to see an empty office just waiting for someone to fill it with office furniture, phones, pictures. And that was only the beginning. I still had to find my first customer, to make my first sale. There was no greater excitement and enjoyment than when that was accomplished—all by myself. It took four months to fill my first job order; I wondered if I would ever make that first sale. I quickly learned patience while I also learned to repair the photocopier, the mail meter, the secondhand typewriters. The little things in life mean a lot to the entrepreneur, who must master them all, especially the art of being chief cook and bottle washer.

Patience

This is the one virtue you are forced to learn in order to survive. It takes a long time to succeed in any new business venture. Problems arise, you find solutions, only to have new problems develop, requiring different solutions. (How do you handle a customer whose bill is long past due, who himself is having problems collecting from his customers?) Sometimes there are no quick solutions, so you try to avoid the problem as long as it doesn't do too much damage. Training new employees takes time and the patience of Job. In our field it takes up to six months to train new recruiters properly before they begin to earn their keep.

Self-confidence

If you decide to go into business for yourself, but you have little self-confidence, don't despair. Confidence grows with your own successes, and can be fueled by adversity as well. You may have suffered a loss of confidence on your present job. Don't carry that into your new venture. Short courses in self-confidence are available in continuing education programs in most cities. Books and tapes on the subject abound. It shouldn't take you too long to gain confidence.

My entire career has been a series of ups and downs in self-confidence, a roller coaster. Changes in confidence come from failures and successes. If you have more individual suc-cesses than failures, you will tend to be more confident, and vice versa. Obviously, you would prefer to be confident at all times, and that should be your daily objective.

From the day I opened the door of my new business, I had no doubt that I would succeed. This feeling carried over into my business development phone calls, so that my potential clients began believing in the superiority of our services.

Take the case of the four business partners who established a small retail container shop in Dallas, Texas, by investing $35,000 of their personal savings. They sold home storage and organizing units, plastic stack-on units, trays, and the like. In eight years they built the business up to five outlets with sales of $12.5 million. They now plan to add three more stores in the next year, to be financed completely from the company's profits. Their confidence in themselves and their product paid off handsomely in the long run.

You must believe in yourself if you want your customers to mirror your enthusiasm. It's difficult to inspire anyone if you don't believe in yourself. Lack of self-confidence is not an illness, but it is a symptom that something is wrong with your attitude. Attitudes, however, can be changed—but only you can change them.

Financial Backing

To start a business, you must have capital. Then, you must have more capital to sustain the newborn endeavor until cash from sales begins to pay off current expenses.

If you have a good personal credit history, you may be able to get a bank loan. I suggest that you develop a three-year business plan, including projected profit-and-loss statements in addition to a typewritten summary of how you will execute your plan. Indicate who in your organization will do what, and when.

You must know exactly how much capital you need to borrow, and you must have collateral to back up your loan. Rehearse your presentation the night before. With your new blue suit and matching tie, you should be beaming with confidence when you see your bank commercial loan officer. If I had it to do over again, this is the route I would take. Although my business did succeed with a personal shoestring investment of $3,000 in 1971, I would have been more successful sooner with a larger capital base.

As it was, I outfitted my first office with used furniture, in a low-rent location. I did, however, have sufficient capital to invest, as well as other offsetting intangible assets that more than overcame my cautious initial investment. Having been an active NAA board member for 16 years, I had made many friends and acquaintances, some in executive hiring positions. These eventually became my clients, and were responsible for my early business successes.

If you have sufficient capital or can reasonably obtain it, you might consider a franchise. The better national franchise chains will train you to run your new business, but they can be expensive. Taking on a partner or partners is another way of developing sufficient capital, but you must choose your partners wisely. Close friends and relatives sometimes make poor partners.

A Broad General Knowledge of How a Business Operates

Accountants generally can make good entrepreneurs because they have a good conception of how businesses are run and what makes them succeed. Your experience as an accountant can be invaluable in running your own business. You can save money by keeping your own books, and you also know the basics of cash control, payables, taxes, inventories, and how these relate to the overall concept of making a profit.

There are many reasons that 50 percent of all new businesses fail in the first year, and they all have to do with inadequate preparation for running a business, which I will not discuss in detail here. Suffice it to say that many businesses do fail simply because their owners never ran a business before.

Before rushing to open the doors of your new business, it would be prudent to take a course on entrepreneurship. Such courses are offered by many colleges and community colleges. Victor Kiam's *Going for It! How to Succeed as an Entrepreneur* (1986) should be a bible for the fledgling businessperson. I also recommend reading *How to Start and Run Your Own Word Processing Business* by Gary S. Belkin (1984), before starting your own business. *Entrepreneuring* by Steven C. Brandt (1982) provides a thorough blueprint for creating a growth-oriented business. It goes into such areas as finding the right partners, defining your product and target customers, handling cash, and other important things to consider in running a new business.

Unfortunately, I had not read a single book on this subject when I made my decision, though I'm sure there were many similar books available in 1971. My business would have prospered faster if I had educated myself first—no doubt about it!

Frank Walker, a 39-year-old CPA, took an accounting background and some personal savings and used the combination to create three growing and profitable Michigan manufacturing companies, with combined sales of almost $10 million. The corporation, which makes junior activewear and sleepwear, started in 1985. In 1984, Walker started Sterling DataPak, which manufactures computer accessories, and Sterling Products, which produces grinders for stained glass makers.

As a young and new entrepreneur, Walker believes there are opportunities everywhere for starting a business and making it succeed. You just have to put yourself there and ask yourself, "Can I make that? Can I market that?" Then apply yourself to making it happen.

Many women in Michigan struck out on their own after hitting a dead end on the corporate ladder, according to a survey released in 1987 by *Michigan Woman* magazine and the accounting firm of Touche Ross and Company. This survey also said that female business owners tend to be self-starters who use their own money to buy their business. The women who responded were, on average, over 35, married, without young children at home, and with an education beyond high school. Twenty percent had college degrees, and 27 percent of those had undertaken postgraduate studies.

The single greatest drawback of being an entrepreneur is the loneliness and isolation of your responsibility. There are no peers with whom to discuss plans, victories, or failures. But the freedom of owning a business is incomparable. You can work as hard and as long as you wish. Much to your surprise, you will discover that you are not infallible when it comes to making decisions. You soon learn to make quick decisions to keep your plans going, even though you may not have sufficient information to make a prudent decision. The words *instinct, guess, feel,* and *confidence* all come into play in making people-related decisions. You soon learn how to be a good salesperson because you sincerely believe in your product and you are sure someone will use your services.

My experience as an accountant prepared me for success as a business owner. My background as a cost, budget, and pricing analyst, and as a controller, for three corporations in three different fields helped me run my employment business on an original investment of $3,000. Knowing about cash control and credit was a big help. Experience on corporate finance staffs taught me to use tact and respect when dealing with businesspeople. I learned how to work with customers, especially those having cash problems themselves. I learned how to deal with borderline unethical customers by letting them "save face" and not confronting them over minor issues.

"The customer is king" is my motto. I have been bawled out by the finest customers in the world. One customer called me all kinds of unprintable names before finally giving me an order. He thought our prices were much too high compared to what he was willing to pay. Eventually, though, we were able to negotiate a price that made us both happy.

What Are the Real Risks?

Since 90 percent of new endeavors do fail, there must be reasons for these failures. Each failure is unique and has different reasons behind it. One reason for failure can be poor timing and lack of capital. Although I succeeded in starting my employment agency during Michigan's recession of 1971, others have tried and failed. A former top employee of mine started her own employment agency during the 1981 recession. She gave it a good try for over a year. Although she was well qualified, lack of funds and cash reserve led to failure as the recession wore on. If she could have gotten beyond the second year, she would probably still be in business today.

"Timothy Sullivan," a CPA, age 34, with eight years experience with four small CPA firms, decided to become a sole practitioner. After eight years his salary was lower than he desired, and he was considered a supervisor but with no one to supervise. A married man with two small children, he concluded he could do better on his own. With his savings, he rented a small suite of offices and purchased furniture on a lease–purchase plan in a Detroit suburb. Although Tim was able to take a few clients with him, they were not enough to cover his expenses when he opened his doors as a professional corporation. Although his accounting GPA at the university had been 3.5, he was not outgoing and had difficulty knocking on doors and cold-calling for new client prospects.

Realizing his dilemma, Tim quickly invested in a Dale Carnegie sales course to help him obtain new customers. He realized that his sales and marketing techniques needed fast improvement if he was to survive. Having good technical skills and good work habits were not enough. He was willing, but he simply did not have enough customers. While Tim was developing these needed sales skills, he solicited the services of his more outgoing wife (a former bookkeeper), who also made cold telephone calls. She was better at it than Tim, but the clients still did not flock in.

Tim had now survived two years of private practice. His wife was able to put in four hours a day as a receptionist/bookkeeper to help while her own mother took care of the children. With perseverance, hard work, and marketing development, this firm may survive, but barely. It may take another two or three years for Tim to be earning as much as he did when he worked for another firm. All-around talent, plus hard work, perseverance, and some luck—that's what it takes to survive. Desire and a dream are a beginning, but not enough.

What are Timothy Sullivan's risks? If his business fails, he can always go back to working for someone else. Four to five years in a new business can mature a young accountant quickly. At age 39, Tim should have no trouble getting a job in the public or even in the private sector. But he would have to give up all that independence, and say, in an interview, that that was all in the past. He went for it—and now his new career is in front of him.

As I've said, being an entrepreneur can be a pretty lonely business. There are no bosses to give you decision-making advice, and many of your accounting friends may not be in a position or have the time to help you. If you can work in such an atmosphere and enjoy it, it's a plus for you in the battle of survival in a highly competitive endeavor.

Nowadays, not only are there plenty of competitors perform-ing the same service as the Sullivans, but there are also many bookkeeping services, as well as other large and even Big Eight firms that are entering the small-client field to give you more competition.

Another caution—should you have a new product or service, believe me, unless you have patent or trademark protection, it won't be long before another competitor or two enters the ring with you. You must anticipate it.

My suggestion is that, if you have entrepreneurial leanings, you go into business as early as possible in your career. The market does allow us some early failures on our career path. Indeed, most successful and street-wise executives know that you must experience failure before you can become successful. I believe this wholeheartedly, and I speak from experience. No one has *only* successful career experiences. People just aren't as quick to tell you about their failures.

Generally speaking, successful accountants become successful entrepreneurs. This doesn't mean that if you aren't or weren't successful in your present job, you would *not* make a successful entrepreneur. You must find out the reason or reasons that your career is not going in the desired direction. Once you have determined that, owning your own business may turn out to be a good idea. For example, if you are not happy with extremely detailed accounting work, but you are doing it just to make a living, perhaps a change is in order. Administrative, analytical work may be more up your alley. I know that in my own career, I disliked actually doing the basic bookkeeping, specifically the debits and credits, closing the books, and so forth. But I did like

analyzing the balance sheet and the financial statements. Therefore, I made sure I moved toward the analytical side of accounting and toward controllership functions. Grunt work, though
necessary for most accountants, was not for me.

☐ SALES AND MARKETING

Accountants who consider changing fields could certainly qualify for careers in sales and marketing. Sales is one field that does
not normally require any formal education. Many larger firms
do require degrees or specific higher level positions, but an
accounting degree would likely be sufficient for most sales and
marketing positions.

Our firm grades the candidates we interview on a scale of 1 to
10 for appearance, intelligence, and personality. Under "personality," we will usually add the qualification "sales-oriented"
when we detect someone who is an unusually good communicator with a strong, forceful command of the English language.
Many managerial and executive candidates have these characteristics and would have little difficulty in switching to sales
work.

Many CPAs also have natural sales abilities, which they use
in auditing and counseling their many clients. Many CPAs have
switched to positions in recruiting, financial planning, computer
marketing, and stock brokerage.

Consider the story of Rick Bloom, who became a CPA in 1978
and, today, is a successful financial planner and a radio celebrity
in Michigan. Rick loves his work, but it wasn't always that way.
It was natural for Rick to enter public accounting, since his
father was a CPA. He started his career with two local CPA
firms, but soon realized something was missing. Debits and
credits, general ledgers and financial statements just didn't turn
him on as he had thought they would. But he did enjoy the
financial planning aspect of CPA work.

Judiciously, Rick analyzed his talents, skills, needs, and
options and decided that earning a law degree and entering the
legal profession could be the way out. He resigned his position in

public accounting and began studying law full time at the University of Michigan. Shortly after his graduation in 1982, he joined a Detroit law firm specializing in estate and financial planning and taxes. Rick liked the work—so much, in fact, that he felt confident enough to join his brother Ken in forming the law firm of Bloom and Bloom, specializing in financial and estate planning.

Several years later Rick's career took another turn. Radio station WXYT had an opening for a host for its highly successful talk show on financial planning, a three-hour, live question-and-answer program broadcast every Sunday. Rick beat out ten other talented candidates for this position.

Thus, at age 33, Rick Bloom, CPA, has successfully experienced four different careers—accounting, law, financial planning, and radio broadcasting—and has been successful in all of them.

To take another example, "Lester Everett," after receiving his accounting degree from Eastern Michigan University, began his accounting career at Burroughs Corporation. Lester was a good accountant, but his heart wasn't in it. He requested a transfer into the marketing and sales department, which marketed accounting hardware and software to the banking industry in and around Detroit. The company sent Lester to in-house courses to make him an expert in selling and developing rapport with bank data-processing executives. The combination of his accounting skills and his ability to learn basic computer languages as well as hardware and software capabilities put Lester into a dual-skill category that gave him career flexibility. When the demand for his specialized product dropped, Lester, at 29, was able to return to accounting, first as a budget supervisor and eventually as controller. But Lester has not really decided what he wants to do. Between jobs, he purchased a training school franchise, which never really succeeded. He gave that up when he went back into accounting. At age 35, after three different careers, Lester is still searching for the ideal one.

Ray Costan had the desk in front of mine at a large corporation's controllers' staff, and we often discussed our dreams and plans. Ray had a BS in accounting from Wayne State University, but it was obvious from our conversations that his great love was the stock market. (His uncle was a stockbroker who had probably fostered this passion in Ray.) Ray, who was married and had young children, decided to leave his job and try his hand as a stockbroker with Merrill Lynch. His assets were his numbers skills and an unquenchable desire to learn all he could about the market. Today, he is a successful vice-president in Kidder-Peabody's Detroit office. When we have lunch together, we exchange thoughts about our success at switching careers. We both agree that we love our second careers and had no difficulty in making the transition.

In 1950, "George Gilliam" was my first accounting professor at a small eastern college. He was an excellent teacher, who was able to maintain my interest in accounting as a major. When I transferred to the University of Detroit, I lost track of George, but in 1972, after I had decided to enter the employment agency field, I ran into him at a NAA meeting in Detroit. George had left the teaching profession and gone to work for a large Michigan corporation as a divisional supervisor of accounting. He indicated that teaching paid so poorly that, despite his love for it, he could not adequately support his family. George missed his students and academia, and industrial accounting just wasn't the same as teaching, but he stayed with it for economic reasons.

For George, both careers had turned out to be failures. But if he had persevered and found a school with higher pay scales, George might have reached his objective.

Career success requires that you choose the right field early enough in life that, if you do need to change careers, you can do so while still at a marketable age. Most accountants are potentially multiskilled—they just don't know it. Their skills are latent; they have been built up over the years and lie in reserve, coming to the fore only when needed.

☐ CONSULTING

Many large CPA firms, especially the Big Eight, employ consultants, who need not be CPAs, although some firms require an

MBA or other master's degree as a prerequisite. A four-year degree with various majors may be required for other specialties.

Some of the consulting these firms perform includes:

Cost accounting

Budgeting

Systems and procedures

Health care

Management information systems

Banking

Statistical analysis

Long-range planning

Retail

Hospitality

Degreed accountants who have specialized in certain industries could qualify for some of these consulting positions.

Other consulting firms, not affiliated with CPA firms, also hire accountants as staff. Some specialize in such areas as inventory control, pensions and profit sharing, self-insurance, asset control, real estate, risk management, and venture capital, to name just a few.

For personal reasons, "Mark Levin" recently resigned his position as a CFO with a real estate development and construction firm. He left with good references after four years, and although local high-paying jobs for CFOs were scarce, Mark was confident about himself and his future. Because he was a Big Eight CPA and had a friend in heavy construction field audits, Mark decided to go into consulting. He and his friend decided to specialize, because they knew both the accounting and the general management side of the industry. Until they were able to develop several clients, Mark did per diem work.

Mark and his partner both work from their home offices; an answering machine was their first out-of-pocket expense. Although they are serious about their future as consultants, they are waiting for a few more clients before they rent an office and equipment. They are not yet too concerned about an office and a professional image—that can come later. But now, after only three months, they have their first problem: How can they service their clients and develop new ones? Word about their good work gets around slowly in the industry. Their marketing plan is a combination of direct mail brochures and cold calls during lunch hour, using their cellular phones and answering machines at home. They plan to take one day between assignments for developing new business. Since both partners are outgoing and gregarious and have networks in their industry, they decided that both would work on new client development, including the necessary grunt work. At this early stage they will accept any assignment, from cost accounting to budgeting, inventory control, taxes, accounting, and management systems. Their first-year income projection for 1988 is $135,000, to match their 1987 combined base salaries.

☐ PUBLIC ACCOUNTING

Most nonpublic accountants know that CPA firms usually prefer to hire potential CPAs directly from college with a good academic background in accounting. There is a certain amount of switching, mainly CPAs with large companies changing to smaller firms for potential partnership positions no longer available in their own firms. Occasionally, CPA firms hire degreed accountants with a short history in industry. The Big Eight firms usually require a 3.0 college grade point average in accounting.

Some smaller CPA firms hire industrial accountants as junior accountants, at a junior accountant's salary. Usually there is a trial period in which these accountants can become certified within a reasonable period of time. Accountants who decide to become CPAs after 15 or 20 years in the industry will have a hard time finding a CPA firm willing to give them a chance— although it's still possible.

Big Eight CPAs are the most sought-after and most marketable accountants in the field. The Big Eight label almost guarantees the high quality of the individual as an accountant, although, as in any profession, there are exceptions. Many of the top financial executive positions require previous Big Eight experience. They are reserved for the cream of the accounting crop. Even small and medium-sized CPA firms have quite rigid specifications for staff positions.

9
ETHICAL CONSIDERATIONS

One of the best deterrents to the new rash of white-collar crime is a "trip to the big rock." That's what former U.S. Attorney General Griffin Bell told NAA members at their June 1987 national convention in San Diego. Bell warned that more and more accountants will be drawn into corporate criminal cases unless they take steps to avoid compromising situations altogether.

Bell, lauding the recent return to corporate morality since the passage of the Foreign Corrupt Practices Act, noted that management accountants will play a key role in discovering any problems with their organizations and reporting what must be done. Take, for example, a former accountant with TRW, Inc., who won a $700,000 judgment against the company in 1987 after convincing a jury that his superiors had ordered him to defraud the government. During the trial, Alan Russ testified that he was fired in 1984 as a part of an internal managerial shake-up designed to convince the federal government that TRW had dismissed employees who fraudulently inflated prices on government contracts, even though the scheme was actually being directed by managers higher up in the company (National Association of Accountants Convention, Newsletter, June 1987, San Diego, California).

Another accountant, José L. Gomez, looked at ethics differently. Gomez, a former managing partner of a Big Ten CPA accounting firm, was sentenced to a 12-year prison term for his role in the fraud of ESM Government Securities, Inc. According to the March 4, 1987 issue of the *Wall Street Journal,* Gomez knowingly approved the firm's false financial statements for five years.

A former bookkeeper is serving two years in prison for embezzling from a fast food firm in Michigan. By juggling sales, payroll, and tax accounts over a three-year period, the employee stole over $1 million.

More than ever before, U.S. businesses are required to meet specified standards of ethical practice. CPAs have a professional code of ethical standards, and non-CPAs should voluntarily uphold these same standards in dealing with corporate financial statements and external reporting to government agencies.

The problem of right and wrong has perplexed philosophers since the time of Socrates and Plato. What counts is what is right for *you*—not for your fellow employee. How much do you owe your corporation? How much are you willing to do to be successful?

☐ NICE GUYS CAN FINISH FIRST

I believe this statement wholeheartedly. There is absolutely no way that unethical activity on the part of an accountant can be condoned. I'm sure it happens—probably more often than we imagine. But the risk and the consequences are so great that accountants should not even be tempted.

Many accountants have confided in me that their superiors recommended they pursue certain unethical and even illegal accounting activities. Usually, by the time they told me about their experience in unethical behavior, they had already resigned or had been dismissed.

I recall my own first confrontation with a question of ethics, many years ago. Upon request from our CPA audit firm, I passed on certain historical accounting records that could have been embarrassing to our management. I was subsequently dismissed for using poor judgment. As it turned out, no one was embarrassed except myself, because I was made to feel I had done wrong in acting honestly.

Should you blow the whistle on a boss who acts unethically, or remain passive and resentful? Obviously, this is a sensitive and potentially explosive situation. To act, you must have documented proof of your superior's behavior. At the same time, in case your allegations backfire, you should begin exploring job openings that may be available to you. Don't confront your boss. Instead, seek out a trusted top executive with your evidence. Remember that committing an unethical or illegal act because your boss ordered you to will not relieve you of liability; you may be prosecuted. If you are fired, and you *do* have proper evidence, you should immediately contact an attorney or your state attorney general's office.

So far, we have discussed only the most serious breaches of ethics, in which you as an accountant may never be tested. However, there are other actions in which we get entangled that will test our integrity. For example:

1. Do you work and produce to your maximum ability, or do you just "fake it"?
2. Do you abuse the use of the company telephone? The company car? Company-paid seminars?
3. Do you overstate your travel and entertainment expense account?
4. Do you keep your word when you make a promise?
5. Do you make up negative stories about fellow employees who are competing with you for the next promotion?
6. Do you play dirty in office politics?
7. Would you lie to your boss to protect your job status?
8. Do you knowingly attempt to undermine your immediate superior's position for your own benefit?
9. Do you lie to your superior and blame shortcomings or errors on your subordinates?

Remember, business ethics and social responsibility are far more important than any immediate gain.

☐ MORAL COMMITMENTS

Ethics or the lack of it reflects enormously on every part of our life. It's the supporting factor in equal opportunity and human rights. Many businesspeople try to rationalize their willingness to do things dishonestly in business, as long as it's "for the good of the company," meaning good for profits. These same business-people can go to church on Sunday and lead a perfectly moral life after 5:00 P.M. and on weekends. But this has to be a contradiction of values. What is needed is a renaissance of ethical standards.

☐ ESTABLISHING A STANDARD OF INTEGRITY

Colleges like the University of California at Berkeley, the University of Pittsburgh, and the University of Washington now make business ethics a required course in their bachelor's and master's degree programs. This is a step in the right direction, but it will be years before it has meaningful results.

There are only two ways to upgrade ethical standards in business. Both employers and employees must voluntarily initiate ethical standards programs. Corporations can offer in-house business ethics courses as a requirement for promotion. Corporations, of course, must operate within federal and state regulations on business behavior. Employees must transfer their personal moral and ethical beliefs to the office, without fear of being ridiculed by their peers or superiors.

Our moral values have been implanted in us since childhood. They come from our home environment, school, peer influence, religious upbringing, and the media. It is very important for us to question them from time to time, to make sure they are based on strong beliefs. Otherwise we may find ourselves confused when we have to make ethical decisions on the job.

The accounting profession needs stricter regulations, and that regulation should come from within the business, not from the government. That is the view of J. Michael Cook, chairman and chief executive officer of Deloitte, Haskins and Sells, one of the nation's leading accounting firms. According to the *Detroit Free Press,* Cook told the Economics Club of Detroit recently that "The accounting profession has been under scrutiny in Washington primarily because the Washington, D.C., Committee on Oversight has linked many of the failures to auditing procedures and has begun asking, 'Where were the auditors?' " As a result, there has been a rush to introduce legislation designed to control fraud in both management and reporting procedures. But such legislation may not be needed, according to Cook, who is also chairman of AICPA. Cook said that the accounting profession has initiated its own projects in response to congressional concerns. According to Cook, these include clarification of professional standards to make it clear that the detection of material fraud is a principal objective of any examination of financial statements.

"Leonard Opal," a CPA who was treasurer for a small auto parts manufacturer, resigned from his firm because he did not want to be involved in what he regarded as unethical assignments from the company president. Although he would not discuss the proposed infraction in detail, as a CPA, Opal clearly knew right from wrong; he had read the rules on ethics for CPAs many times. Opal, whose salary base was $60,000, called me to ask for job assistance. He said he would get good references from his employer. I got him one interview for a CFO position at a higher salary. My client never raised to me the ethics question that was discussed in the interview. It was not a factor in the decision to hire Opal; experience and personal chemistry were.

Since the question of ethics is so sensitive, word getting back to the company could have opened up all kinds of litigation, particularly if Opal's statement wasn't 100 percent accurate. Most of my clients would not probe the ethics question too deeply if they were convinced the applicant was sincere and was telling the truth.

Applicants, even if pressed for more specific detail about the unethical behavior of a former boss, should not reveal all the sordid details to the prospective employer. An applicant who tells too much could, in fact, be deemed unethical for doing so, because of the need for absolute confidentiality in the client–CPA relationship.

One thing is sure: The prospective employer will be fairly certain that this new employee won't stand for any unethical nonsense on the job. And that could scare off some quasi-unethical, self-made corporate presidents who have gotten away with such behavior over the years.

Many people think business managers should be more ethical than they are. This whole issue of ethics is a gray area, with no clear definition of right and wrong.

Companies have responsibilities to stockholders, employees, communities, and the government. Sometimes they find it difficult to balance all those obligations. Businesspeople have the same human weaknesses as anyone else and should be judged accordingly. Is it fair for a company to take advantage of an employee in order to show a higher profit? Conversely, is it proper for an employee to spend excessive time avoiding work? Does "ethics" lie in the eyes of the beholder?

10

CHANGING CURRENTS IN THE ACCOUNTING FIELD

Since 1950, when I was graduated from college, tremendous technological, sociological, and political changes have occurred that have affected the accounting field. Everything has changed—how accountants do their work, what they think about their profession and corporate life, and how they plan their accounting career. In recent years, U.S. corporations have picked up some Japanese management techniques to help them function more efficiently.

What the Japanese learned from U.S. industry after World War II was the Industrial Revolution all over again. The concept of efficient operation—tight middle management—is not really new. The Japanese knew that if they copied U.S. technology and work habits (efficiency), they would never be able to undersell anybody. In automobile manufacturing, for example, the Japanese, not having a strong automotive union like the United Auto Workers (UAW), could easily install tougher production schedules with fewer managers at much lower pay scales. That wasn't done overnight; it took over 30 years for the Japanese to perfect their system. Meanwhile, U.S. automakers' payrolls and materials costs were skyrocketing, while the U.S. automakers produced only an adequate quality automobile.

In the past few years, not only has the auto industry gotten on

165

the "tightening middle management" bandwagon, so did the rest of U.S. industry. Since most white-collar workers are not unionized, this has been an ideal spot for industry to cut costs. This phenomenon has affected middle management accountants, and will affect them significantly in the 1990s. Up to now, accountants had been accustomed to the pyramid principle of promotion—plenty of rank and file, with a few at the top. In the 1990s, we can look forward to more and more people at the bottom, fewer and fewer at the top. Reorganizations, acquisitions, and the forming of megacorporations all mean fewer corporate positions for top echelon financial executives, and more and more plant, divisional, and subsidiary accountants with fewer and fewer corporate spots to be promoted to. What will happen to all the talented middle management accountants? They will reach a plateau sooner than their parents did.

☐ EFFECT ON UNDERGRADUATE EDUCATION

Up to now, colleges did an excellent job of churning out technically equipped accountants for U.S. industry. But what colleges are doing now will not be good enough for the future because of the tremendous changes in the making. U.S. college administrators should be planning their 1990 curriculum as soon as they can, before it is too late to do the accounting college graduate any good. The undergraduate of tomorrow not only should learn the principles of accounting, as well as auditing, costs, and the usual technical curriculum, but must also take other relevant practical courses in order to survive the 1990s and 2000s. What kind of courses do I have in mind? For the undergraduate, they might include the following:

1. "Principles of interviewing": The majority of accountants have not developed a good interview technique. Many supervisors and managers do not know the basics of interviewing and selecting good people.
2. "Strategy for Finding a Job": After quitting or losing a job,

many young accountants have difficulty setting up good job search programs.

3. "Keeping Your Job": Many accountants could have avoided losing their jobs by following simple procedures that can be taught.

4. Accountants will be reaching a plateau earlier in their careers than their predecessors did. Courses on plateauing should be offered.

5. "Principles of Job and Life Wellness": Many accountants are still unaware that the quality of their home life directly affects their behavior on the job, just as job satisfaction affects behavior at home. The realization that there can be a common ground for both may offer new insights into a better job and home life.

☐ EFFECT ON GRADUATE EDUCATION (MBAs, MSTs, AND OTHER DEGREES)

We can expect to see more and more accountants entering master's degree programs to prepare themselves for the fierce competition of the future. The following courses should be added to the master's programs:

1. "Career Planning (Short- and Long-Range)": Many master's graduates feel that completing such a program constitutes career planning. It does open many doors. But what happens when those doors close? A new plan must be made.

2. "Introduction to Japanese": More and more Japanese companies are investing heavily in new corporations in the United States. Many economists feel that eventually there will be greater interdependence between Japanese and U.S. industries. A knowledge of Japanese culture and business will better prepare accountants for the future.

3. "Entrepreneuring": With earlier plateauing, more and

more accountants may want to go into business for themselves. These courses will prepare them to succeed against great odds.

4. "Advanced Computers": Most accountants complete only the basic computer courses required for a degree. The accountant who has a superior computer education, however, will move up the ladder more rapidly. Colleges must offer more advanced computer courses related to accounting and advanced finance. Large accounting staffs will be displaced by more powerful computers that will be available to executives. Accountants must be trained to use these computers effectively.

11

GREATER DEMAND FOR CONTINUING EDUCATION

☐ A WIDER FIELD OF COMPETITION

Accounting has in recent years welcomed an increasing ratio of minority practitioners. More women are currently earning accounting degrees and certification than men, and racial and ethnic minorities have earned a full spectrum of professional positions in major firms and private practices. The requirement of continuing education has widened the starting gate in the race for managerial and controller positions. The contenders are more numerous, and ambition for promotion has to be matched with provable knowhow.

☐ CHANGING TAX LAWS

Constant changes in corporate tax laws are making tax returns so complicated that the average accountant has not been able to keep up. Even CPAs must take extensive tax courses just to be able to communicate. Practicing tax specialists must continue to take these courses forever. There is good evidence that more accountants are entering master's in taxation programs.

As corporations become more complicated through mergers

and acquisitions, there is a greater need for accountants to be familiar with the international, pension and profit sharing, and SEC aspects of taxation.

☐ UPGRADING OF SKILLS (CMA, CPA, CIA, CFA)

I know of a young, talented banking executive who is a CPA, a CMA, a CIA, and an MBA. From an educational standpoint, he is well prepared for the future. You can never have too much education, as long as it's relevant to your career advancement.

There are a number of better jobs developing that require both a CPA certificate and an MBA. More and more job specifications call for CMAs or CIAs. If I had it to do over again, I would take the time to earn an MBA. More and more, education makes the difference between promotion and being passed over. That's why it's a good idea to get your advanced degrees early in your career. All extra accounting education is basically good, of course. But waiting to get your master's in the twilight of your career, though it may make you smarter, will not make you any more marketable.

☐ COMMUNICATION IMPROVEMENT COURSES

Experts in executive recruiting place a high value on an accountant's ability to speak well. The further away your job is from manual work, the more important it is for you to be able to convey your thoughts effectively in speaking. The ability to express yourself is probably the most important nontechnical skill you can possess. It must be part of your career game plan.

Top managers have told me that the ability to communicate was a most important executive trait. I have met many brilliant accounting technicians who, in important staff meetings, suddenly become tongue-tied buffoons.

To overcome a fear, do what you fear most. I always thought that phrase was invented exclusively for me. Early in my life, and through college, I developed all kinds of communication problems and fears. Raised in an ethnic family atmosphere and neighborhood setting, attending a parochial elementary school,

I was never sure which language to use. As a result, in high school and college I was reluctant to answer questions, even when I knew the answers. I was even asked to take a remedial English course. (Fortunately, I did much better on written exams.) Most accountants can probably trace their communication skills, or lack thereof, to earlier stages of development over which they had little or no control.

Looking back, I am certain that a lack of good communication skills slowed down my career progress at a giant corporation, where there was an abundance of accounting talent and plenty of competition. Realizing this, I began the slow uphill battle. I took the free in-house courses in "Comprehensive Reading" and "Public Speaking." These courses helped in the short run. There is a tendency not to retain knowledge gained from quick self-help courses unless you apply it immediately to everyday activity and develop new habits that supersede old ones.

Reaching the prime age of 35 as a financial analyst, I had come to a plateau without realizing it. The word *plateau* was not in my vocabulary. All I knew was that I was bored with my assignments and my career appeared stalled. Perhaps I rationalized a bit, but at this point I labeled myself a "late bloomer" and theorized that if only my communication skills were upgraded to the level of my analytical skills, I could begin moving up in my career.

Psychologists say that acknowledging your faults is half the battle. The other half is doing something about them. This is the more difficult half, since you must enter uncharted waters, where things can get uncomfortable.

The public speaking course was an eye opener for me. My improvement was slow, almost undetectable. Should I keep taking this same course over and over again just to maintain the slight gains I had made in communication?

Fortunately I read an article about the Toastmasters organization in a national magazine. As soon as I joined the Toastmasters Club nearest to my home, I realized that this was going to be extremely hard work, since I feared speaking in front of groups larger than two.

Perhaps my fear wasn't much different from that of Thomas A. Murphy, retired chairman of General Motors, whose nervousness before giving a speech was so strong that it almost made him physically ill. As a true leader, however, he accepted public appearances more than once a week.

I did not enjoy my weekly attempt to become articulate. Getting up several times each meeting was difficult enough, but the one-minute extemporaneous talk was pure torture for me. I dreaded coming to these meetings because they quickly revealed how poor a speaker I was, or thought I was. I could virtually hear the snickering in the audience, and I seriously thought about quitting. As I looked around the table, however, and listened to other frightened speakers, I soon learned that we all had the same problems and the same objectives. We were there to help each other become better communicators. We came from all walks of life—a treasurer of an insurance company, a budget-planning executive, a Chrysler Corporation engineer, a salesman, a controller, a lawyer and politician, a banking executive, and so on.

It definitely was not a social club, since we had weekly speaking assignments and followed an excellent textbook program, which became more difficult with each chapter. The average Toastmaster remained a member for about a year, leaving as soon as he became proficient. I stayed for five years because my progress was painfully slow. It was several years before I began enjoying the club. Eventually, however, I reached the end of the rainbow when I entered the Annual Toastmasters' Speech Contest, became club champion in 1964, and advanced as far as the district finals. Winning this speech contest brought me new confidence and improved self-esteem.

My career began changing for the better about that time, too. Late in 1964 I was offered a controller's position with a fine company. I soon joined professional accounting organizations and accepted accounting seminar chairmanships. I became active in professional organizations where I practiced my public speaking at regular board meetings. Over the years I was asked to give formal speeches at various NAA chapters, at colleges, and eventually at the annual Michigan Bar Convention.

Do what you fear to do—that advice was a blessing in disguise for me, and it can be for you as well. Communication skills can make the difference between success and failure in your career. Evaluate your skills, and then act. You can learn how to make what you say count. Successful accounting executives have been using "power" language to get results for years. By becoming a more effective communicator, you increase your ability to influence your subordinates, your associates, and your superiors. You learn how to hold your own in debates during staff meetings and, above all, learn when to stop talking and begin listening.

☐ COMPUTER COURSES

Although most colleges have offered computer courses for a number of years, older accountants and executives, because of their advanced position, may have bypassed the all-important tool of computer literacy. Lack of computer knowledge may not have hurt their careers so far, but eventually it may. I know of many unemployed financial executives who have had difficulty in finding new jobs, mainly because of their lack of experience in electronic data processing (EDP).

In many corporations or divisions of large plants, the EDP responsibility rests with the controller or the CFO. That's why it is imperative to gain as much experience as possible in this field. This does not mean becoming a programmer or systems analyst but, rather, taking basic courses in computers. Learning to use Lotus 1-2-3, Symphony, and other similar programs is a must for accountants. Effective cash management, budgeting, pricing practices and strategies, business planning, and graphics can quickly be mastered using Lotus 1-2-3 applications.

None of us wants to become "obsolete" in our field. Yet many accountants are slowly becoming extinct because they are not continuing their education or updating their technical skills in a society where technology changes in every generation. Nine out of ten job openings that our firm receives from corporations call for varying amounts of computer knowhow.

Late in 1987, "Johanna Salerno" was not offered a position as senior accountant because she had no direct personal computer (PC) experience, even though she had had several basic computer courses in college. Although she was a very capable accountant, her first after college had been as office manager/bookkeeper for an old-line architectural firm that still did its accounting manually. Johanna's lack of experience with Lotus 1-2-3 spreadsheets prompted the company to hire someone else who had *less* pure technical experience.

Johanna should have been more discerning about her first job. She should have questioned the use of an antiquated accounting system and its impact on her own future. I recommended she register immediately for PC, Lotus, and Symphony classes. Her next prospective employer may be even more demanding about computer knowledge and skills.

One small pharmaceutical client, seeking a supervisor of accounting, was not as demanding of computer experience. The controller indicated that if candidates had had basic computer courses in college, and had general computer knowledge, they could pick up Lotus 1-2-3 on the job. The company would underwrite the cost of evening classes for computer courses.

Nowadays, with computer technology changing rapidly, candidates for the top financial positions (treasurer, controller, CFO) who lack extensive EDP experience will not survive. And although knowledge gained from computer courses does not count as actual experience, it's the next best thing.

Suppose you are too busy to take time off to attend college classes. NAA offers a series of independent self-study programs for accountants who must master Lotus 1-2-3. The Micro Mastery Series provides everything accountants need to know about spreadsheets, databases, business graphics, and microcomputers in a convenient self-study format that emphasizes interaction between the computer, an audiotape, and a workbook. Participants will solve real applications problems and develop practical models using Lotus. They will compare their work to printouts of spreadsheets, files, and graphs.

☐ JOB ENRICHMENT COURSES

Most accountants, once they have landed a job, begin a time-consuming process of improving their job performance by trial and error. What they desperately need is a "job enrichment" plan that teaches them the skills necessary to maintain a successful accounting career. A career without regular training and updating sessions is like a ship without a rudder, unable to reach its destination through shifting currents.

Many young accountants in the late 1980s think about their jobs and life-styles differently than their fathers did 20 or 30 years ago. Problems that are regularly analyzed today—getting along with the boss and the client, handling petty jealousies, playing corporate political games—were of little interest in the Eisenhower era. Accountants may have griped about these problems, but they were unlikely to discuss them openly or make them an issue at management seminars. Company loyalty was greater in those days; employees didn't need to be motivated constantly to work productively for their employers.

Over the past two decades, expectations at the workplace have changed, with a growing emphasis on interpersonal relationships relative to technical skills. To sum up these current expectations: To prepare young managers for the twenty-first century, you have to teach them things that are important in human relationships—understanding how to work in groups, how to listen, how to care—and how to share the fact that they care. The need to be a cog in the giant wheel of a CPA firm or corporation also has evaporated. Many companies have managers who are more concerned with their leisure time than with life from 9:00 to 5:00.

"The degree of your accomplishments [at work], whether you're a chief executive or a clerk, doesn't designate your success," says Tom Russell, chairman of the board of Federal-Mogul Corporation, a Fortune 400 metal products manufacturer. "It's whether or not you're happy in what you're doing and doing it with enthusiasm" (*Today*, Winter 1984, p. 207).

The only way for young and old accountants alike to assimilate these newly desired abilities is through job enrichment courses and seminars. You can learn new techniques for controlling your emotions, acting like a boss, or improving your listening ability, just as you can learn to type or speak a foreign language. For some accountants, in fact, these techniques are like a foreign language. The more you practice, the more you hone your job enrichment skills.

"People problems" on the job have turned many promising careers around. Solutions to these problems don't come from textbooks or from well-meaning friends. Only sharply focused courses will help. Like any good refresher course, these classes should be taken over and over again.

When we see a well-executed play in a close professional football game, we seldom realize how much time and effort that team has expended in practicing the play over and over again. Even these accomplished professionals, who already know their trade, must rehearse continually to do a good job. Accountants should follow their example.

The following is a list of subjects that accountants with varying degrees of experience might consider when planning their job enrichment programs. Each addresses an important aspect of work that is often overlooked.

Defeating a Negative Personality. The single most important cause of executive failure is an abrasive personality. You may need a course in body language to overcome this personality flaw. Some executives have a natural talent for poking others in an irritating, sometimes painful way. But anger and abrasiveness only communicate that something is wrong. Encouragement with a kind word or smile is a much more effective teaching device than punishment with a frown. A negative personality may have worked for J. Edgar Hoover or Richard Nixon, but it probably won't work for long nowadays.

How to Listen Effectively. This should be a top-priority course for accountants. Corporations are full of bosses and subordinates who simply do not listen attentively. Many people, instead of concentrating on what is being said, are thinking about what they are going to say next. Inattentiveness breaks down the lines of communication and leads to a failure to carry out important instructions.

Listening takes deep concentration. The necessary techniques, unfortunately, are not taught in colleges. Some companies, for example, deal with this issue by offering in-house courses on listening.

Coping With On-the-Job Jealousies.   Unresolved jealousy on the job can destroy careers. Jealousy takes many forms, but it is the common denominator among such types as the martyr, the overcompetitor, the tyrant, and the motivater. Jealousy is a predictable side effect when businesses promote competition by fostering a hectic and sometimes cutthroat environment.

Handling Anger.   Psychotherapists have described anger as an explosive feeling that, if unexpressed, turns inward to create such disorders as ulcers, heart attacks, headaches, overeating, and colitis, not to mention the havoc wreaked upon work relationships. A trained psychotherapist, psychiatrist, or businessperson turned educator can apply work-related criteria to a classroom workshop on anger.

A useful book on this subject is *Anger: The Misunderstood Emotion,* by Carol Tavris (1982). Tavris covers these points and others, such as the problem of angry executives who can only express themselves by attacking and belittling others. This is certainly an area where many accountants need help.

Looking and Acting Like a Boss.   Debra Benton, managing partner of Benton Management Resources in Denver, Colorado, offers a course called "Executive Presence" in which executives are taught a sense of bearing and personal magnetism that hits others before they even open their mouths. In a staff meeting or a reception, the moment a CFO or a partner enters the room, you know that this is the person in charge. They project themselves through appearance, gestures, pace, posture, poise, and demeanor that makes the impression. At first they're acting the part, but before long they become the part.

The course is divided into minuscule subcategories of behavior.

1. Walking into the room (pausing for a second)
2. Standing erect (West Point cadet look)
3. Eye contact (looking at people like a hunter after prey)
4. Gestures (painting pictures with your hands)

Each point may seem insignificant, but, combined, they create images that make people take notice.

Many courses of this nature are being initiated by adult education and private firms in response to the needs of accountants and financial executives. Accountants must look at their education as a never-ending process to meet the pressures of competition and the needs of a fast-moving and rapidly changing national economy.

Walk Like a Thoroughbred.   How does top management form their opinions of us?

1. By what they *see*—our *personal appearance*
2. By what they *hear*—our *speaking voice*
3. By what they *feel*—our *personality*

Then, each of us has a real opportunity to do the things that will assure accountants of *gaining favorable attention*.

Consider the first subject: what people *see* in us.

How do you walk? Does your posture denote real pride, self-confidence, spirit, and good breeding? *Do you walk like a thoroughbred?* Make a date with a full-length mirror and see if what you *see* suits you.

Will you see your head set on top of your spine, making a straight, flat back? Or is it a turtle neck, with the head running out of the upper chest? Is the chest up and out, with shoulders down?

Here are a few briefs on *posture* that will give you top scores.

1. Put your weight on the balls of your feet—use your heels to balance.
2. Tuck in your derrière.
3. Flatten your abdomen.
4. Pull away from your spine.
5. When you rise out of your chair, say to yourself, "Belly up."

☐ BUILD YOUR LIBRARY TO REINFORCE YOUR GAME PLAN

For some accountants, education ended with college graduation and their first job in accounting. For the ambitious, however, those steps are only the beginning. College prepared you for your career. Your formal postgraduate education (MBA, MST, and so on) gave you an edge over your competition. Your informal postgraduate education should sustain your career and keep it from stagnating and unraveling through your retirement. Part of your informal postgraduate education should include reading and extracurricular studying to keep pace with changes in accounting and management techniques.

Every accountant should have a personal business library. My own library includes about 300 books on management, accounting, executive development, job hunting, and related business subjects. I have carefully picked topics and books appropriate to career planning. These sources also provide useful research material for my third career, business writing.

The *Wall Street Journal* and the business section of your local newspaper should be your daily required reading. Make the time to read at least three nonfiction business-related books, like *Iacocca*, Denis Waitley's *The Joy of Working,* and Richard N. Bolles's *What Color Is Your Parachute?* Get them as soon as they reach the bookstore shelves. This will keep you up to date on what the rest of the country is thinking about in the business world.

Your library should begin with reference books such as:

The Accountant's Handbook by Lee J. Seidler and D.R. Carmichael (Ronald Press)

Accountants' Cost Handbook by James Bulloch et al. (Ronald Press)

Don't throw away all your dusty college textbooks. They can also be quick reference tools. Remember that reference books really are meant to be used for *reference.* I don't expect you to read these reference books from cover to cover, but you can use them to brush up on standard costs or operations research when necessary.

Many accountants have not developed a day-to-day planning system. They go to work, they do their job, but the responsibility of planning their career is left to the company. If you are allowing this to continue year after year without taking charge of your own career planning process, you may suddenly and unexpectedly find yourself obsolete.

Annual diaries or similar planning guides should be used in conjunction with your annual career review day. On that day, you can log in your plans for career improvement over the next 12 months. This could include self-improvement courses planned, book and magazine subscriptions needed, association meetings and conventions, and the like.

The psychological advantage of using a diary to record your career plans is that you commit yourself in writing to a program of self-improvement. Thinking about self-improvement without following through is a waste of time. Keeping a diary converts dreams into plans and helps you transform plans into actual effort. Then you review your plans and your effort. This is a sound approach, one that I still use to plan my own career and my business so that I remain current and competitive.

Vocabulary and Reading.   How many new words did you learn in the past year—5, 25, or maybe even 100? Even if you learned 500, any normal 6-year-old child has you beaten. The average 4-year-old knows 5,000 words, the average 9-year-old 30,000. That's a gain of 5,000 new words a year.

Vocabulary development should be a lifelong process. Words can release your positive or negative energy. Educational research points to a definite connection between vocabulary and success. But unless you suffer from insomnia, don't try studying and memorizing long, tedious lists of unfamiliar words. I've tried it—it's a waste of time. The best way to enlarge your vocabulary is simply to read, and read widely. As you come across unfamiliar words, you'll find that you can get the meaning of many of them by the way they are used. Read with a red pencil in your hand, underlining the important passages so you can quickly review the heart of the book.

Use Your Other Two Vocabularies. In all your speaking—social, business, and civic—you are only as good as your basic tool— your vocabulary. Many books have been written on ways of increasing your word power. In essence, we have three distinct vocabularies: verbal, written, and reading.

Our *verbal* or speaking vocabulary is by far the smallest. These are the words we use in business conversations. In speaking, for example, we might say, "There's no explanation." Your *written* vocabulary is larger. In writing the same thought, we might say, "It is inexplicable."

Look at some of your letters and reports; you will find scores of words that you use in *writing* that can be added to your speaking vocabulary. You already know the meaning and correct usage of these words.

Your *reading* vocabulary is your largest. This includes not only the words you speak and write, but also hundreds of other words you recognize and understand when you see them in context, but would be unable to define if you were asked their actual meaning. This vocabulary is harder than your written vocabulary to integrate into conversation. But the battle is half won, since you do know the approximate meaning of these words. Expose yourself to good reading material, something other than mass circulation magazines and newspapers.

Your writing and reading vocabularies are already a part of you, waiting to be put to use for better business communication. I have known hundreds of accountants who have obtained better jobs because they had excellent vocabularies and used them skillfully. This translates into good verbal communication knowhow.

In my interviewing rating system, I particularly look for applicants' ability to express themselves. People with a large verbal vocabulary have more descriptive words to choose from in making business points. That gives an accountant more power in passing on technical accounting information to others.

Of course, your vocabulary must be business-oriented. Often the seeds of a promotion are planted in staff meetings. Good vocabulary must be conveyed in a confident manner for this skill to become meaningful. In 1955, "Edward Tollamar" had a very good vocabulary. The price analysis section of a large division brought Edward in from a competing auto firm to become a supervisor. It was obvious his communication skills were superior to those of others on the staff, although his technical accounting skills were only average. He quickly moved to higher positions within the division as he parlayed his communication skills into productive alliances. He then left the company for out-of-state controller and CFO spots. Then, in 1986, I saw Edward Tollamar's picture in a Detroit business magazine; he was negotiating with presidents of firms his company was considering acquiring, and eventually he became president of a growing multiplant conglomerate. Edward's vocabulary, verbal communication, and interpersonal skills were his greatest assets. What does this indicate? A top executive needs not only technical skills but also good communication as a vehicle in which to convey this talent.

12

MEMBERSHIP IN PROFESSIONAL ASSOCIATIONS

Strange as it may seem, membership in professional associations is not for every accountant—although it should be. Logically, you would think all accountants would consider their profession the greatest on earth and would back that up by active participation as a member. But it's not true. Not everyone has the same level of ambition. Not all accountants have the drive, energy, and pride required for such active participation. *Apathetic* is, unfortunately, the word that describes many accountants of this generation.

American businesspeople, including accountants, are so busy being affluent that they sometimes overlook the value of membership and participation in professional associations. Active association attendance in recent years has decreased significantly nationwide as other interests—television, family, sports—have become more important than active association membership. Participation in those personal events does not call for sacrifice; they are pleasurable in themselves. But it does take sacrifice to succeed in business. Participation in professional associations develops positive habits that can easily be transferred to the business world. Ambitious accountants need every bit of help they can get to carry their career forward in the desired direction.

☐ AICPA: AMERICAN INSTITUTE OF CERTIFIED PUBLIC ACCOUNTANTS

The certified public accountant (CPA) designation requires a four-year college degree, two years' experience in public accounting, passing a five-part national exam, 40 hours of continuing professional education (CPE) annually, and licensure by a state board.

Typically, AICPA speakers discuss such areas as financial and tax planning, ethics, health care, federal and state tax updates, detecting fraud, governmental accounting, legal considerations, and auditing. Other benefits to members are:

Subscription to a monthly magazine, the *Journal of Accounting*

Social events

Active committee participation, which develops leadership abilities

Contacts with prospective business clients

An annual meeting and convention

Potential employer/employee contacts

A speakers' bureau

Personality and public speaking development in committee meetings

☐ NAA: NATIONAL ASSOCIATION OF ACCOUNTANTS

Founded in 1919, shortly after World War I, the NAA is entering its seventieth year with over 90,000 members in more than 350 chapters worldwide. NAA's membership comprises men and women representing a wide variety of occupations, including corporate officers, executives, auditors, controllers, and accountants in industry. Many CMAs, CPAs, and CIAs are also members of the NAA and fill high offices in the association. Some of the advantages of membership are:

Excellent monthly technical speakers

A chance to meet other accountants with similar problems (I

often call fellow members when I have technical accounting problems I can't solve.)

Subscription to a monthly management accountant magazine

A chance to develop public speaking expertise in board meetings as a committee member

Development of ethical standards

Employment services at the local chapter level

Periodic newsletters

The CMA (certified management accountant) designation after taking a comprehensive examination and meeting specific educational and professional standards

Research (The association conducts a continuing program of research in accounting, and the results are published and made available to members.)

As a member of NAA for over 25 years, I can honestly say that as I progressed from member, to associate director, and eventually to chapter president, I also progressed in my career. The network of friends and associates that I developed helped me when I faced difficulties in my own career. Twice I found controller positions directly through the efforts of members who attended the monthly association meetings. I often hear of other accountants who have had similar experiences. Many associates eventually became clients of the recruiting firm I founded in 1971. With encouragement by chapter board members, I took on the job of newsletter editor and director of manuscripts. In 1968 my article on "Standard Costs" was published in the November issue of *Management Accounting,* a national accounting journal. To write it, I learned a lot about cost accounting by researching and analyzing various cost systems.

Active NAA members have many opportunities to practice public speaking and develop communication skills. Technical seminars give members opportunities to express themselves publicly and to gain technical knowledge. I started attending professional seminars and later became a seminar leader and then seminar chairman. Years later I was asked to be a featured speaker at every chapter in southeastern Michigan, and in 1986 I was a main speaker at the Young Attorney's Seminar at the Michigan Bar Association annual convention.

As team captain of the Detroit chapter of NAA, I had the opportunity to work with people like Thomas Russell, now chairman of the Federal Mogul Corporation, who still takes time to speak to NAA chapters occasionally.

John C. Arme, a CPA and managing partner of the San Diego office of Arthur Anderson, was also president of NAA for 1987–1988. He says that "The experience I have had working with groups of people, I believe, really benefited me in progressing with Arthur Anderson. Public speaking and confidence in being able to speak came about because of my participation in NAA."

☐ AAA: AMERICAN ACCOUNTING ASSOCIATION

Next to the NAA, the AAA, founded in 1916, is the organization most focused on the overall development of cost accounting. AAA is open to anyone interested in accounting. It is particularly interested in accounting theory, research, and all phases of accounting education. It publishes a quarterly journal, *Accounting Review*.

☐ IIA: INSTITUTE OF INTERNAL AUDITORS

Originally founded in 1941, the IIA publishes a quarterly magazine, *The Internal Auditor*. The designation of CIA (certified internal auditor) is sponsored by this organization, which has chapters throughout the nation.

☐ AFP: ACCREDITED FINANCIAL PLANNER

Available only to CPAs through the Colorado Society of CPAs, this accreditation involves a six-hour exam plus annual CPE (continuing professional education) and experience in the area of financial planning.

☐ CFP: CERTIFIED FINANCIAL PLANNER

This certification follows a two-year study program with six sections of study, each equivalent to three semester-hours of college credit offered by the College of Financial Planning. Recently, candidates taking courses offered by other educational institutions and approved by the College for Financial Planning, have been made eligible to sit for the exams and obtain the CFP designation.

Other professional associations available to accountants include:

National Association of Hotel Accountants

National Association of Black Accountants

American Society of Women Accountants

Federal Government Accountants Association

Institute of Newspaper Controllers

The American Women's Society of CPAs

Municipal Finance Officer Association

National Association of Bank Auditors

EDP Auditors Association

Tax Executives Institute

American Association of Cost Engineers

13

PUBLIC, PRIVATE, AND TEACHING CAREERS

☐ PUBLIC ACCOUNTING AS A CAREER

Public accounting, as I see it, is a blue-chip, glamorous industry. It shed its green-eyeshade, pencil-pusher image some time ago, for a number of reasons.

Rigid Requirements

Most graduate accountants would like to become CPAs, but the educational, character, and work requirements are rigid and unyielding. Therefore, many settle for non-CPA careers.

At almost all CPA firms, interviewing and selection are geared toward eventual CPA certification and, ultimately, partnership. There seems to be no long-term role or successful future for the less dedicated accountant who cannot pass the required CPA exams or handle the rigorous demands of growing with the firm from junior to senior member, to supervisor, manager, and eventually partner. Obviously these criteria apply to medium-sized and large firms. The smaller, one- or two-person firms also have demands, but personal chemistry and personality fit are the key.

Personality Traits

Many studies have been made of the type of personality that is suitable for the CPA profession. Some say there is a difference between those accountants who work for Big Eight firms and those who decide to work for smaller firms. There is also a difference between male and female personality traits, as well as between tax specialists and staff auditors. Finally, there are differences between managers or partners and staff people.

I generally perceive CPAs' skills and personality traits as follows:

Large Firms	*Smaller Firms*
Aggressive, confident	Not as aggressive (outwardly), but confident
Objective, impersonal	Objective, but personal
Able to use good practical judgment	Able to use good judgment and insight
Practical	More practical
More analytical	Analytical
Figure-oriented	Figure-oriented
Sophisticated	Natural
More scholarly	Scholarly

Public accounting prepares you for many other potential careers, should you decide to do something different later on. With advances in computer technology, major CPA firms will have smaller staffs in the future. The detail work that new public accountants now do will involve less "number crunching." But it will take a more qualified accountant to analyze and supervise a more complex audit.

Women as CPAs

A 1983 survey of 11,000 members of the American Society of Women Public Accountants shows that nearly 70 percent of female CPAs are under 30, and more than 60 percent are employed by CPA firms. Most of the rest are in privately held businesses, largely their own. More and more women are entering the public accounting profession.

Female accounting majors have higher GPAs than their male counterparts. The public accounting industry has done a fine job of assimilating women as employees—and as bosses.

Private industry has been a bit slower in accepting female accountants as equals, but more and more plant accounting departments are hiring female CPAs for plant cost and budget analyst and supervisory positions, with no serious problems attributed strictly to their sex.

Many CPA firms had been concerned about motherhood, clients' acceptance of female CPAs and managers, office romances, and potential travel and entertainment problems. But there is little evidence that these have been serious problems. One Detroit area Big Eight firm hired 30 to 50 percent women for its staff in 1983. This also meant that 30 to 50 percent of prospective male accountants sought work elsewhere, perhaps in smaller CPA firms or in industry. The male–female competition is just beginning to heat up.

Communication Shortcomings

Reading, writing, and arithmetic used to be all our parents needed to master to succeed. CPAs had to know their arithmetic and accounting; the colleges made sure they mastered those skills before graduation.

But reading and writing—communication skills—also need to be developed by accountants. Whether the large CPA firms or the CPAs themselves should take the responsibility for teaching these skills is debatable. One thing is sure, though—with the current trend for clients to sue CPA firms for various reasons, it's imperative that CPAs master both written and oral skills. Writing to a CPA client is a serious task. Unclear evaluation and description of the financial statement could damage a client–CPA relationship.

Yet some potential CPAs still come out of school with little skill in the arts of speaking and writing. Oral and writing courses could be included in the 40-hour CPE requirement. Colleges could add these courses to their curricula and could set up adult education courses. But this could take years. How can young CPAs find out if their communication skills need honing?

In the annual evaluation, supervisors should include an evaluation of both writing and speaking skill. The subordinate then should make it a priority to develop those skills with workshops, seminars, or classes directed toward that end. This education becomes part of the CPA's short-term career planning—that is, if he or she plans to progress and eventually become a partner.

☐ PRIVATE ACCOUNTING AS A CAREER

Most professional accountants who are not career CPAs make their living, as I have, in private accounting. Unlike public accounting, private accounting has no rigid minimum requirements. The term *accountant* is used very loosely in private industry; some bookkeepers and nondegreed accountants still call themselves "accountants." Some large corporations use the title "accountant" for pay grade purposes, even though formal education is not a prerequisite.

Many of the faster track accounting positions, however, require accountants to have at least one degree in order to be considered for promotion. Larger corporations are more likely than smaller ones to care about good grades and advanced degrees from top schools. As a credential, the "school of hard knocks" is slowly becoming obsolete.

Accountants have long been tapped for top corporate posts. Lynn Townsend, a CPA from Touche Ross, ran Chrysler Corporation during my nine years with that firm. Ford Motor Company in 1987 promoted its chief financial officer, Allan Gilmour, to executive vice-president.

If you would like to advance in private accounting, you may wish to become a certified management accountant (CMA), a title created by the National Association of Accountants (NAA).

According to Dr. James Bulloch, CMA, CPA, and managing director of the Institute of Certified Management Accountants, CMAs are management accountants or financial managers who work as inside accountants for an organization and have distinguished themselves by earning the CMA designation.

Unlike a CPA, who works for a public accounting firm, a CMA

generally works for a single employer, which is not an accounting firm. CMAs are found at all levels of management accounting and financial management. Some CMAs hold the positions of controller, CFO, or CPA firm partner. CPAs who have also taken and passed the five-part CMA examination (which must be accomplished within a three-year period) admit that the CMA examination is every bit as difficult as the CPA exam.

Many companies are beginning to recognize the importance of the CMA designation, and are willing to pay for the review courses and examination fees through educational reimbursement programs. Once the CMA certificate is earned, the CMA becomes a member of the Institute of CMAs. CMAs, like CPAs, continue to meet the educational requirements to maintain their certification in good standing. Ninety hours of continuing education are required in each three-year period after passing the initial exam.

If you are an accountant, and you are not a CPA, MBA, CIA, or certified information systems associate (CISA), then the CMA designation would be worthwhile for you to pursue. It may help you stay competitive in a field where the talent becomes better with each passing year.

In 1972, when he decided to take the CMA examination, Joseph A. Mazur was audit manager with Ernst & Whinney, a Big Eight CPA firm. Even though he had earned an MBA in 1965 from the University of Michigan, Joe thought it would be beneficial to test his ability to retain and use the concepts he had learned in college and in his public accounting career. He passed all the parts of the exam in one sitting, adding the certified management accountant designation to his list of achievements and qualifications.

In 1976 Joe accepted an offer to join the Manufacturers National Bank of Detroit, one of his audit clients, as a vice-president and deputy controller. In 1977 he became the controller of the bank and, after several promotions, also became controller of the parent company, Manufacturers National Corporation, in 1982. He has been a senior vice-president since 1983. The corporation grew from under $3 billion in total assets in 1976 to over $9 billion at the end of 1987.

In early 1988, when I asked Joe how the CMA designation had helped his career, he replied, "Preparing for the CMA examination reinforced my understanding of managerial accounting concepts and assisted my ability to deal with the broader aspects of the controllership function." He added: "There is much more to the decision-making process of any financial manager than merely the tax and external reporting issues that are an outside CPA's major concern. I feel that the effort put forth to become a CMA and knowledge gained from preparing for the examination directly benefited me in my approach to my job."

As a strong supporter of the CMA program, Joe was instrumental in initiating a liberal CMA tuition reimbursement policy within his department. In 1985 he hired Manuel Steffas, an MBA from Case Western Reserve University who was also a CMA. Joe was impressed that Manny had the ability to pass the CMA examination and had made the effort to do so. Today Manuel Steffas is a key officer in the management accounting section of Joe's department. Manny also commented, "Studying for the CMA helped reinforce many of the concepts I originally learned in school."

Bob Stoner was already a vice-president of finance of Kelly Services, a leading national temporary employment firm, when he decided to earn a CMA certificate. Bob says the test has intrinsic value because it takes a certain amount of intelligence, determination, and management accounting knowledge to prepare for and pass it. In Bob's position, he hires many managerial accountants and will often consider CMAs over non-CMAs when reviewing résumés. Bob indicated that the computer division of one giant firm lists the CMA certification as a prerequisite for certain management positions. Many manufacturing corporations now add the CMA requirement to their job description for jobs that previously required only CPA certification.

☐ TEACHING AS A CAREER

Tony Lee, staff writer for the *National Business Employment Weekly,* had a February 1984 article headlined "Faculty Shortage Severe at National Business Schools." The demand for qualified business professors, he stated, continues strong in all disciplines, according to reports from the American Assembly of Collegiate Schools of Business.

Salaries for business professors rose to an average of $35,000 for the 1983–1984 terms, while business school deans earned $54,100 on average. Exhibit 13.1 gives some idea of relative salaries in the field.

Executives interested in pursuing a college teaching career should first consider the following issues:

The peculiarities of teaching

The disparity in salaries from institution to institution, as well as geographically

The disparity in qualifications (some accounting schools require CPA or MBA accreditation)

The relative pressure and freedom involved in teaching

An accountant who is considering an academic position as a career change, should probably first consider a part-time or temporary position. Some CPAs in private practice have daytime teaching assignments and are able to work around their normal public accounting duties.

Graduate business schools have declared that seasonal executives are highly desirable candidates to fill teaching positions. About 60 percent of the faculty hold PhDs, and 40 percent are "fixed-term faculty" who begin one-year contracts that are

EXHIBIT 13.1 Salary Comparisons, 1983–1984, Accounting Assignments versus Administrators at Public Colleges

Salaries for Accounting Assignments	
Professor	$40,800
Associate professor (5 or more years' experience)	$33,600
Assistant professor	$28,800
New doctorate	$34,000
Salaries for Administrators at Public Colleges	
Dean	$53,600
Associate dean	$47,900
Assistant dean	$37,400

Note: Applying a 5 percent annual increase would reasonably accurately update these statistics.

typically renewed for three- to five-year periods. Some accounting professors can teach until they reach age 70.

For the mature accountant who doesn't really want to retire, but must because of company policy, teaching offers a rewarding career alternative. What could be more appealing for closing out an accounting career than the thought of ivy-covered buildings and the opportunity to offer your accumulated years of knowledge and experience to the eager minds of students. Teaching can indeed be a rewarding career.

Full-time teaching will offer a lower salary than an industrial career, but you can offset that somewhat by consulting or writing books. Also, there's another trade-off—less pressure, which could be very appealing for those who have burned out on fast-track business careers.

Smaller colleges tend to put more emphasis on teaching than on research. Also, these colleges have more time to do consulting and use their teaching staff for these assignments.

To learn more about teaching accounting as a career, I relied on my network of friends and acquaintances at NAA. Lou Petro, dean since 1979 of the School of Management at Lawrence Institute of Technology (LIT) in Michigan, was my target. His enthusiasm is clear evidence that this man loves his job. But Lou didn't start out in the teaching profession. He began his professional career as a registered mechanical engineer, working for General Motors. While working on his MBA program, he developed an affinity for accounting—he found the accounting courses a snap. He broke into academia in 1969, teaching accounting part time at LIT. He subsequently taught accounting full time at the University of Detroit, my alma mater, and was then offered a manager of MIS position with Alexander Grant (now Grant-Thornton) in Chicago, where he worked for three years, obtaining his CPA certification in the process.

Not only did Lou make a good transition from engineering to public accounting, he then made an equally good transition from accounting to college teaching. Three major career changes—yet on the way he also found time to become a CMA, a CIA, a CISA, and a PhD. Whatever education Lou needed, he quickly obtained.

Lou told me that an MBA and/or a CPA would be a desirable qualification for someone interested in teaching at LIT. A PhD would be necessary to teach graduate-level courses. If you're considering teaching as an alternative career, examine your early thoughts about teaching. Also review the courses you like the most in high school and college.

Lou indicated that there is a serious shortage of accounting teachers in the cost and managerial accounting, advanced costs, accounting information systems, and EDP auditing areas.

In Michigan, it's possible to obtain a CPA certificate without having any actual public accounting experience. You still would have to pass all parts of the CPA exam. Obtaining a master's degree in accounting allows you to skip one year of CPA firm accounting experience. Teaching accounting courses in college can be substituted for another year, and two years of experience working for the IRS would let you skip two years of CPA experience for obtaining a CPA certificate.

Teaching part time can offer many personal and developmental rewards, says "Dan Olstein," a CPA and financial executive who teaches accounting at Macomb Community College.

1. It develops organizational skills—each day's lecture must be planned ahead of time.
2. It develops a teacher's technical knowledge—students' questions necessitate further research and study.
3. There's personal satisfaction in seeing faces light up when the students finally understand the answer to a particularly difficult accounting problem.
4. The part-time teacher has a chance to test the teaching profession before actually getting into it full time.
5. Teachers learn about human nature from their students and get an idea of the direction the country is going.

☐ MOONLIGHTING

Moonlighting refers to the practice of holding a second regular job in addition to one's main job. It requires plenty of energy, stamina, and determination, but it can be an excellent way for an ambitious accountant to earn more money, learn another career, or start a new business.

My only experience in moonlighting occurred shortly after my graduation from college. My first experience with a recession came when I was looking for my first accounting job. Times were so tough in 1950 that I had to settle for an inventory control position. Since this wasn't exactly the accounting career I had in mind, I moonlighted. I took on an evening position as book-keeper/office manager for a small engineering firm, in order to get some badly needed accounting experience. (The extra money also came in handy.) My regular job ended at 4:30 P.M., and my evening job ran from 6:00 P.M. until midnight. Being single and full of ambition and incentive, I was able to keep up this grueling pace for about six months.

Moonlighting to Earn More Money

From a career planning standpoint, it makes sense if the money earned is to be used to advance your own or your spouse's career, or to start a new business. This approach to accelerating your business career will require superior planning so that you don't burn yourself out. Recharging your batteries between jobs takes a tremendous amount of discipline, as well as proper rest and diet. But it can be done if you accept that the sacrifice of your free time is not wasteful. Once you have determined that moonlighting is necessary for your career, mind control must take over. Self-motivation and concentration are necessary to keep you going when the going gets rough. If moonlighting begins to hurt your main job, you had better review your financial needs again and determine whether it's worth the risk to continue.

Learning Another Career

It's always a good idea to test out a potential alternative career. Moonlighting is one way to do this without waiting years to find out if the new career is for you.

If your second job happens to be in EDP, for example, and you're getting hands-on programming and systems experience with another company, this plan seems sound. Chances are that your main employer would not approve of your moonlighting within the company. They probably would not like the idea of your working at two jobs.

Starting a New Business

If you were planning to start a CPA practice in the evenings while working for a large corporation or a CPA firm, moonlighting is a way to start this venture. At first, until you develop your client base, the demand on your evening time will not be great. If your partner works full time developing new clients, as well as doing some of the accounting, then you can do the rest of the grunt work in the evenings and on weekends. As your client base grows and your new venture requires more of your time, perhaps the time will come to quit your main job and devote yourself full time to the new business.

Should you desire to become a tax specialist, it might be wise to work for a small CPA firm in the evenings, or to develop a tax client business in the evenings and on weekends during tax season. Then you would be moonlighting only during tax season.

If you are not a CPA and you are interested in moonlighting, personal income tax service is the easiest and quickest field to break into. It's a natural for any accountant because it requires a minimum of training and cash outlay. You will need an annual brushing up on new tax laws and revisions. You can begin your new endeavor by preparing personal tax returns for your family and relatives, free of charge. This will give you a chance to get familiar with the new tax forms and develop speed in filling out the forms. Then approach your friends, neighbors, and acquaintances. You'll have to market your services and fees, perhaps using a low-cost direct mail program, such as sending out flyers. Make sure your rates are somewhat lower than those of the franchise firms. Placing ads in church newsletters and local newspapers will help you develop new business. Begin early in the year. At the same time, you can approach H.&R.

Block, Nationwide, and other national franchises for part-time work. Some small CPA and bookkeeping firms also seek tax preparers during the tax season.

Don't be too eager to quit your main job until you are absolutely sure you and your business partner are compatible. As with a marriage, it takes some period of close contact to learn each other's shortcomings and peculiarities; incompatible personal and business habits may not become irritating at first, but they may, later on. You need ample time to reflect on whether being an entrepreneur, with that particular partner, is for you.

In all these cases, if you have a family, it is imperative that you discuss your moonlighting plans with your spouse before you start. It will mean almost constant absence from the family. All family members must be encouraged to cope with this temporary situation in the hope that it will be beneficial for the entire family in the long run.

Single people may have more independence in the use of extra time, but they too must have a strong enough character to sacrifice their social life during this period. Success seldom comes without some sacrifice or risk.

Many accountants moonlight for any of the three reasons mentioned earlier. For some, it's really a matter of family survival. For others, it's a way to upgrade a family's economic status. For still others, it's a method of testing a new career or entrepreneuring.

Even though I have moonlighted, I question the logic of professional accountants doing this simply for financial reasons. If it's for family survival, then moonlighting may be necessary. But my experience tells me it's almost impossible to serve two masters adequately. Your full-time job will eventually suffer, and that's your breadwinner—and also your profession.

Your moonlighting job probably will not require as much concentration as your full-time job. From a long-range career-planning standpoint, it probably would be more prudent actually to take courses to upgrade yourself so that you will become a better employee, thereby justifying a higher salary from your full-time employer. Taking computer courses or courses earning you an MBA or CMA will eventually influence your superior to upgrade your salary. More concentration and better execution of your function on your present job will reap accolades and eventual monetary rewards.

Self-improvement courses in confidence building, better listening, faster reading, and public speaking will also do more for you in the long run than moonlighting will to improve your full-time job performance and earnings. The courses will become a permanent investment in your future, whereas moonlighting generally is only temporary.

☐ PLANNING YOUR RETIREMENT

"Martin Brown" was a dynamic CFO who managed his finance department with forcefulness and success. He was instrumental in turning an unprofitable multiplant plastics manufacturing firm into a very profitable, growing one. At 45, he became controller, at 50, treasurer, and then, at 57, chief financial officer. Martin drove himself hard until he was 62, when he was forced to retire because of company policy. Within six months, Martin had died of a heart attack.

Thousands of accountants face the same situation as Martin Brown. He was very successful in his career but totally unprepared for the demands of retirement. I have consulted with hundreds of accountants, and over and over again I hear the same complaint: "Retirement wasn't like I thought it was going to be."

Many about-to-retire accountants dream of moving to the sunny beaches of Florida or California, or the hot, dry sunshine of Arizona, only to find that kind of life more boring than they ever imagined. How can a hard-driving accountant who has, for 45 years, used the hours from 9:00 to 5:00 for useful activity suddenly get used to a sedentary life of leisure? No matter what changes you make in life, you must be retrained—nothing comes automatically. Even retirement must be planned, and you must train yourself for this new way of life.

The postretirement period can become the most important period of your life. That is why your career plan must include the postretirement period—in writing, revised annually on your birthday.

The dangers facing many retiring financial executives must be brought to their attention. They may face emotional upheaval, domestic problems, and depression due to the inability to find meaning in a life without a job.

Retirement can be what you make it. It can be fantastic and memorable, or dull and forgetful. Your plans for the future must be well defined. Going to the sunny beach day after day will soon become boring if you're going to do it for the rest of your life. If you live in a place like Hawaii, where the sun always shines, you may begin to look forward to cloudy or even rainy days. Many prospective retirees put too much emphasis on the physical aspects of retirement—enjoying the sun, sleeping late, and the like—and not enough on how they will occupy their minds once they get up and begin each day.

In any other culture, this probably would not be a problem, but American culture has conditioned us to believe that we must be doing something useful and beneficial to society. There's a tendency for retirees to feel useless. Close companionship helps but probably is not enough in itself. Independent activity and use of your mind and your skills are needed, too.

I know of one CPA who retired with his wife to some lovely acreage in the Southwest, only to return to Michigan to be near his extended family. He got involved in many civic and social activities, but for some, even this would not be enough.

As an entrepreneur, I plan to work as long as I am able—as long as my health holds out. I hope I have the presence of mind and the wisdom to know when the time for retirement is right. Every year, near my birthday, I will consider my plans for the next three years. I used to make a five-year forecast. When the time does come, I will not just retire. I will cut back to four days, then three, two, and finally one. As I wind down my activity in business, I will take on more writing activity. That is my plan.

Accountants planning retirement and beyond can consider:

1. Starting your own bookkeeping or CPA firm
2. Purchasing and arranging a fast food establishment

3. Consulting on a per diem basis
4. Getting into politics (One accountant friend of mine successfully got involved in local city politics, from which he also derived some retirement income.)
5. Working for civic groups
6. Working for charities
7. Managing condominiums or a retirement home
8. Doing per diem work for a CPA firm
9. Owning or working for an employment agency specializing in accounting
10. Teaching
11. Volunteering at your church
12. Running seminars on financial topics (taxes, estate planning, and the like)
13. Doing free-lance writing on corporate subjects
14. Selling real estate
15. Managing your own investment portfolio
16. Turning a hobby into a business (coin collecting, flea market or antique sales, music, appliance repair)
17. Taking special courses (literature, travel, writing, foreign languages)
18. Joining a book or literary club
19. Joining a garden club
20. Joining and becoming active in professional associations

Industrial psychologists and management consultants should put in more research time in finding new ways to tap the potential of retiring accounting executives. Colleges and corporations should begin offering courses and in-house programs to prepare retiring accountants for their future. I can foresee a new industry developing that will teach people about to retire how to take care of themselves physically and mentally after age 55. I can foresee new degrees being offered—retirement consultant, retirement engineer, and so on.

In 1987 there were about 41 million people in the 50-to-75 age group. By the year 2000, there will be 59 million. As the average life expectancy of U.S. citizens goes higher and higher, the need grows for special services for the 55-and-over population. Some services have not yet been invented, but many enterprising large corporations are already including this age group in their marketing plans and programs.

I believe many corporations are missing a fine opportunity to harness the talent and resources of the 55-plus age group. This is largely a matter of reeducation and evolution.

At age 55-plus, an employee probably has accumulated more knowledge and wisdom than younger employees. Industry today is geared to youth. But it should be sophisticated and adaptable enough to make room for both youth and age. Solving the retirement problem *is* possible—if it is taken seriously by the powers that be.

Where would McDonald's and other fast food corporations be today, if a retired person had not taken hold of a hamburger store and developed it into a gold mine? Who knows what a retired accountant can dream up and develop into a profitable, worthwhile endeavor. Retirement need not be the end of the road. It could be the beginning of a fabulous adventure.

14

CONCLUSION

Few things in life are more important than your career. Your job labels you; it defines who you are. It determines your life-style and your social status. Yet the chances are good that, up to now, you have spent very little time or energy planning your career.

It is never too late to begin planning your career and developing career advancement skills. It doesn't matter if your career has only recently been launched, or if you are at a dead end, or if you are approaching retirement age. Career planning should go on forever. In my thirty years as an accountant and a recruiter, I have observed and experienced accountants' lives and have counseled many accountants who, through annual planning, have turned their jobs into happy experiences, even if they did not reach their original goal of CFO or company president.

Hard work alone will not guarantee job success. But annual reevaluation of your career—in writing—allows you to keep adjusting positively to different circumstances (promotion, demotion, marriage, death in the family, divorce, children). Reevaluation minimizes your chances of developing a "comfort zone" that can hurt your career. If you stop to evaluate where your career is at the end of each year, and where it appears to be going, you are in a position to alter your circumstances should you so desire. With a lifelong career plan, you can minimize the big surprises, the hills and valleys, and can maintain greater control over your destiny.

In many ways career planning for accountants is like a journey down a great river. There are stretches of quiet water and gentle currents, when the skies are cloudless, the air is bracing, and travel is relatively trouble-free. You skim along between clearly defined river banks with a sense of purpose and progress. Then suddenly, the river broadens and forks, and you find yourself puzzled by backwaters and bayous that beckon you away from your clearly charted course.

Something like this is almost certain to happen in the course of your career. You will surely face a period of questioning, reevaluating, and exploring possibilities for change. Questions will arise about your career and, more generally, about the meaning of life—about whether your expectations are being met. This is the time to work out the flaws and limitations in your design for career and for living.

One morning you will awaken wondering about the hopes and dreams that once brought excitement to your career and to your life in general. When that happens, give yourself the time and the psychological space to rework your design for career and personal life. This transition period offers an invitation to individual growth. Caution is in order: Your career plan and home life may not enter this transitional period simultaneously. They may be out of step. Awareness and understanding are imperative.

REFERENCES

"Alumnus of the Year, Tom Russell, C'48." *Today* (University of Detroit), Winter 1984.

Belkin, Gary S. *How to Start and Run Your Own Word-Processing Business.* New York: Wiley, 1984.

Brandt, Stephen C. *Entrepreneuring: The Ten Commandments for Building a Growth Company.* New York: New American Library (Mentor), 1982.

Eliot, Robert S. "Right Attitude Seen as Key to Beating Stress." *The Macomb Daily,* January 25, 1982, p. 8A.

Ellis, Albert, and Knaus, William J. *Overcoming Procrastination.* New York: New American Library (Signet), 1979.

Iacocca, Lee. *Iacocca: An Autobiography.* New York: Bantam Books, 1984.

Kelly, J. Patrick, and Strawser, Robert H. *Management Accounting,* March 1982.

Kiam, Victor. *Going for It! How to Succeed as an Entrepreneur.* New York: New American Library (Signet), 1986.

Labus, Henry. "The Fusion of Cost Accounting and Industrial Engineering." *Management Accounting,* November 1968, pp. 57–59.

Labus, Henry. "Enriching Careers through Courses." *National Employment Weekly,* April 12, 1984, p. 25.

Lee, Tony. "Where the Jobs Will Be Nine Years from Now." *National Business Employment Weekly,* August 3, 1986, p. 18.

Levinson, Larry. *Executive Stress.* New York: Harper and Row, 1964.

Panyard, Christine M. "Change and Stress." *Michigan Bar Journal,* June 1980, p. 340.

Peale, Norman Vincent. *Enthusiasm Makes the Difference*. Englewood Cliffs, N.J.: Prentice-Hall, 1967.

Safran, Clair. *New Ways to Lower Your Blood Pressure*. New York: Simon and Schuster, 1987, pp. 109–110.

Scott, Beverly. "Stress and Management." *Oakland County Bar Association,* January 1982, p. 17.

Tavris, Carol. *Anger: The Misunderstood Emotion*. New York: Simon and Schuster, 1982, pp. 25–44.

INDEX

Accomplishment
  and career change, 121–22
  enjoyment of, entrepreneurship and,
    144–45
Accountants' Cost Handbook, 179
The Accountant's Handbook, 179
Accounting
  private, as career, 192–94
  public, as career, 189–92
    change to, 157–58
    rigid requirements of, 189
Accounting assignments, salaries for,
  195
Accounting field, changing currents in,
  165–68
Accredited financial planner (AFP), 186
Acquisition of company, 137–40
Acting like boss, 177–78
Age, and stress, 28
American Accounting Association (AAA),
  186
American Assembly of Collegiate Schools
  of Business, 195
American Institute of Certified Public
  Accountants (AICPA), 27, 163,
  184
American Management Association, 119
Anger, handling of, 177
Anger: The Misunderstood Emotion, 177
Annual updating of résumé, 110
Appraisal, fear of, career change and,
  124
Associations, professional, membership
  in, 183–87
Attention, gaining favorable, 178

Backing, financial, entrepreneurship and,
  147–48
Balancing home life and career, 9–20

Birthday
  as designated annual career planning
    day, 109–18
  planning for next, 115–18
Body maintenance, 30–31
Boss
  coping with, 38–42
  expectations of, 44–50
  looking and acting like, 177–78
  marital problems of, 17
  new, 39–42
  older, 43–44
  younger, 42–43
Burnout, and career change, 121
Business
  battlefield of, 3–4
  knowledge of operation of, entrepre-
    neurship and, 148–50
  starting new, moonlighting and, 199–
    201

Cardiac counseling, competing and, 23–
  25
Career
  learning another, moonlighting and,
    198–99
  private accounting as, 192–94
  public accounting as, 157–58, 189–92
  recessions and prosperity and, 18
  teaching as, 194–97
  See also Job *entries*
Career change(s)
  in midlife, 137
  non-necessity of, at plateau, 98–100
  question of, 119–40
  specific, 141–58
  time to consider, 120–27
  weighing factors in, 103–7
Career life, balancing home and, 9–20

Career planning, 1–7
Career planning day, designated annual, 109–18
Cautious personality, 80
Certified financial planner (CFP), 187
Certified information systems associate (CISA), 193, 196
Certified internal auditor (CIA), 5, 99, 111, 170, 184, 186, 193, 196
Certified management accountant (CMA), 5, 111, 117, 170, 184, 185, 192–94, 200
Certified personnel consultant (CPC), 94, 133
Certified public accountant (CPA), 5–6, 19, 23, 26, 69, 92, 94, 99, 105, 106, 123, 130, 133, 134, 142, 144, 149, 151, 153, 154, 155, 156, 157, 159, 160, 163, 169, 170, 175, 184, 186, 187, 189–92, 193, 194, 195, 196, 197, 199, 200, 202, 203
Change(s)
  of career, see Career change(s) in life, 135–37
Changing currents in accounting field, 165–68
Changing tax laws, 169–70
College of Financial Planning, 187
Commitments, moral, 162
Communication improvement courses, 170–73
Communications shortcomings, of CPAs, 191–92
Company
  acquisition of, 137–40
  traveling for, 12
  as time-waster, 70
Company culture, matching of style with, 22–23
Competition
  art of, 21–53
  cardiac counseling and, 23–25
  greater field of, 169
  stress and, 25–33
Computer courses, 173–74
Computers, personal, 173–74
Confidence, 46–47
  development of, 48–49
  entrepreneurship and, 146–47
Conflict, mastering art of, 13–15
Consulting, career change to, 155–57
Continuing professional education (CPE), 184, 186
  greater demand for, 169–82

requirement of, 191
Coping
  with boss, 38–42
  with older boss, 43–44
  with on-the-job jealousies, 177
  with younger boss, 42–43
Courage, 45–46
Courses
  communication improvement, 170–73
  computer, 173–74
  job enrichment, 174–78
Creativity, planned, 83–84
Culture, company, matching of style with, 22–23

Daily goal-setting success, and reduction of stress, 29–30
Dale Carnegie courses, 35, 37, 46, 48, 97, 115, 117, 151
Daydreaming, about another profession, 126–27
Deadline pressure, 32–33
Decision making, scheduling of smart time for, 57–59
Defeating negative personality, 176
Demand for continuing education, greater, 169–82
Detail, prisoner of, 64
Discipline, 12
Discussion
  of job, negative, career change and, 125–26
  of personal development, with manager, 110–12
Divorce
  career and, 16–17
  and reactive planning, 5
Dual-career family, 14

Earning more money, moonlighting and, 198
Education
  continuing, greater demand for, 169–82
  graduate, changes in, 167–68
  undergraduate, changes in, 166–67
Effective listening, courses in, 115, 176
Electronic data processing (EDP), 14, 82, 173–74, 187, 197, 199
Emotional ability for career change, 122–23
Emotional outlets, 31
Enjoyment of hard work and accomplishment, entrepreneurship and, 144–45

Enthusiasm, 47–48
"Enthusiasm," 47
Enthusiasm Makes the Difference, 48
Enterpreneuring, 149
Entrepreneurship, 143–53
    risks of, 150–53
Ethical considerations, 159–64
Evaluation, honest talent, 95–98
"Executive Presence," 177–78
Executives
    midcareer
        motivation and, 81–82
        plateau of, 97–98
    older
        motivation and, 82–83
        plateau of, 98
Experienced accountants
    motivation and, 80–81
    plateau of, 96–97
Extinction, avoidance of, 4

Family
    dual-career, 14
    input of, job demands and, 11
Favorable attention, gaining of, 178
Fear of appraisal, career change and,
    124
Field of competition, wider, 169
Financial backing, enterpreneurship and,
    147–48
Foreign Corrupt Practices Act, 159
Forty Plus Club, 132
Future
    jobs in, 18–19
    of promotions, 2–3

Gaining favorable attention, 178
Game plan
    basis for, 6–7
    library and, 179–82
Goal orientation, 49–50
Goal-setting, daily, success in, and reduc-
    tion of stress, 29–30
*Going for It! How to Succeed as an En-
    trepreneur,* 148
Gossip, office, as time-waster, 70
Grade point averages (GPAs), 151, 191
Graduate education, changes in, 167–68
Growth, personal, and career change, 106

Habits
    positive, development of, 37–38
    rest and relaxation, cultivation of, 30
    work

change in, emotional problems and,
    16–17
    for lifetime, development of, 63–73
Happiness, and career change, 123–24
Hard work and accomplishment, enjoy-
    ment of, entrepreneurship and,
    144–45
Home life, and career, balancing of,
    9–20
Home-office-play (HOP) performer, 13
Home relationships, relocation and, 15
Honest talent evaluation, 95–98
"How to Develop the Power of Enthusi-
    asm," 48
*How to Start and Run Your Own Word
    Processing Business,* 149

Iacocca, 179
Ideal job, elusiveness of, 18
Income, need for more, and reactive plan-
    ning, 5
Individualism, 70–71
Information, accumulation of relevant, in
    problem solving, 75
Institute of Certified Management Ac-
    countants, 192
Institute of Internal Auditors (IIA), 186
Integrity, establishment of standard of,
    162
Involuntary job loss, 129–30

Jealousies, coping with on-the-job, 177
Job(s)
    demands of, family input and, 11
    as fact of life, 17–20
    in future, 18–19
    ideal, elusiveness of, 18
    loss of
        involuntary, 129–30
        and reactive planning, 5
    negative discussion of, career change
        and, 125–26
    outgrowing of, 102–3
    preservation of, sacrifice and, 10–11
    stimulation of, and career change,
        105
    See also Career *entries*
Job change, *see* Career change(s)
Job enrichment, 78–79
    courses in, 174–78
Job stress, 25
Job security, and career change, 106
Journal of Accounting, 184
The Joy of Working, 179

Laws, changing tax, 169–70
Learning another career, moonlighting and, 198–99
Library, and game plan, 179–82
Life, changes in, 135–37
  and reactive planning, 5
Lifetime, work habits for, 63–73
Listening effectively, courses in, 115, 176
Long-Range Forecasting, 111
Looking like boss, 177–78
Loss
  of job
    involuntary, 129–30
    and reactive planning, 5
  of promotion
    and career change, 123
    and reactive planning, 4–5
Lotus 1-2-3, 111, 117, 173, 174
Loyalty, to company, 12

Management Accounting, 26, 185
Management Development Course, 115
Management level, and stress, 28
Manager, discussion of personal development with, 110–12
Marital problems, of boss, 17
Marketing, career change to, 153–55
Master of Business Administration (MBA), 5–6, 19, 26, 40, 64, 85, 89, 111, 123, 133, 144, 167, 170, 179, 193, 194, 195, 197, 200
MST, 167, 179
Meetings, as time-wasters, 66–67
Membership in professional associations, 183–87
Micro Mastery Series, 174
Midcareer executives
  motivation and, 81–82
  plateau of, 97–98
Midlife crises, 135–37
  and reactive planning, 5
Modeling, 111
Money, earning more, moonlighting and, 198
Moonlighting, 197–201
Moral commitments, 162
Motivation, 78–79

National Association of Accountants (NAA), 26, 36, 69, 99, 117, 131, 132, 148, 155, 159, 172, 174, 184–186, 192, 196

Need
  for more income, and reactive planning, 5
  for respect, 79–83
  for self-esteem, 79–85
Negative discussion of job and profession, career change and, 125–26
Negative personality, defeating of, 176
Networking, 131–32
New boss, handling of, 39–42
New business, starting of, moonlighting and, 199–201

Office gossip, as time-waster, 70
Older boss, coping with, 43–44
Older executives
  motivation and, 82–83
  plateau of, 98
On-the-job jealousies, coping with, 177
Operation, business, knowledge of, entrepreneurship and, 148–50
Opportunistic personality, 80
Opportunity, promotion, and career change, 104–5
Outgrowing job, 102–3
Outplacement, 129–30
Overtime, right amount of, 11

Paperwork, as time-waster, 68–70
Patience, enterpreneurship and, 146
Peers, unhappiness of, career change and, 124–25
Persistence, enterpreneurship and, 145–46
Personal appearance, 178
Personal computers (PCs), 173–74
Personal development, discussion of, with manager, 110–12
Personal growth, and career change, 106
Personality, 178
  defeating negative, 176
Personality traits, of CPAs, 190
Phone calls, as time-wasters, 67–68
Plan
  of action, in plateau situation, 95–107
  game
    basis for, 6–7
    library and, 179–82
Planned creativity, 83–84
Planning
  career, 1–7
    designated annual day for, 109–18
    erroneous, 6

for next birthday, 115–18
  reactive, 4–6
  retirement, 201–4
Plateau, in career, 87–107, 171
  acceptable, 91–92
  non-necessity of changing career at,
      98–100
  plan of action at, 95–107
  unacceptable, 92–95
  and career change, 121
Positive habits, development of, 37–38
Positive thinking, 35–38
  course in, 115
Posture, 178
Power drivenness, 50–53
Premature comer
  motivation and, 80
  plateau of, 96–97
Pressure, deadline, 32–33
Previous year, review of, 112–15
Prisoner of detail, 64
Private accounting, as career, 192–94
Problem solving, 73–78
  accumulation of relevant information
      in, 75
  examining and choosing most logical
      solution in, 76–77
  noting of possible solutions in, 75–
      76
  putting solution to work in, 77–78
  recognition and definition of problem
      in, 74
Procrastination
  motivation and, 84–85
  and stress, 31
Productivity, time of
  most identification of, 55–57
  important work, at, 30
Profession
  daydreaming about another, 126–27
  negative discussion of, career change
      and, 125–26
Professional associations, membership in,
      183–87
Professional designation, acquisition of,
      and reactive planning, 5–6
Promotion(s)
  future of, 2–3
  loss of
    and career change, 123
    and reactive planning, 4–5
  opportunity of, and career change,
      104–5
Prosperity, and career, 18

Public accounting, as career, 189–92
  change to, 157–58
  rigid requirements of, 189

Quality of work life, 9–13

Reactive planning, 4–6
Reading, vocabulary and, 180, 181
Recessions, and career, 18
Recruiters, 132–34
"Red-circling," 88
Relaxation habits, cultivation of, 30
Relocation, and home relationships, 15
Resignation, 127–35
Respect, need for, 79–83
Rest habits, cultivation of, 30
Résumé
  annual updating of, 110
  as security blanket, 112
Retirement, planning of, 201–4
Review, of previous year, 112–15
Risks, of entrepreneurship, 150–53

Sacrifice, job preservation and, 10–11
Salary(ies)
  for accounting assignments, 195
  and career change, 104
Sales, career change to, 153–55
Scale of Life Events, and stress, 27
Security, job, and career change, 106
Self-confidence, 46–47
  development of, 48–49
  entrepreneurship and, 146–47
"Self-Confidence," 46–47
Self-esteem, need for, 79–85
Self-sabotage, success, 100–102
Skills, upgrading of, 170
Slenderization, 3
Slippage, avoidance of, 4
Smart time
  scheduling of, for decision making, 57–
      59
  taking charge of, 55–85
Sophomore
  motivation and, 80
  plateau of, 95–96
Speaking voice, 178
Speed Reading, 115
Standard of integrity, establishment of,
      162
Starting new business, moonlighting
      and, 199–201
Status, and career change, 107
Staying with job, 103–7

Stress
  and competing, 25–33
  daily goal-setting success and reduc-
    tion of, 29–30
  job, 25
  overreaction to, 32
  reversal of, 34–35
  Scale of Life Events and, 27
  in subordinates, minimization of, 33–
    34
Style, matching of, with company culture, 22–23
Success in daily goal-setting, and reduction of stress, 29–30
Success self-sabotage, 100–102
Symphony, 111, 173, 174

Talent evaluation, honest, 95–98
Tax laws, changing, 169–70
Teaching, as career, 194–97
Temporary positions, 134–35
Time
  allocation of, with spouse, 14–15
  most productive
    identification of, 55–57
    important work at, 30
  smart
    scheduling of, for decision making,
      57–59
    taking charge of, 55–85
Time hoarding, 65–66
Time-wasters, handling of, 72–73
Toastmasters International, 85, 97, 115,
  117, 171–172
Tough Times Never Last, but Tough Peo-
  ple Do!, 90
Traveling for company, 12
  as time-waster, 70

Undergraduate education, changes in,
  166–67
Unhappiness of peers, career change and,
  124–25
United Auto Workers (UAW), 165
U.S. Bureau of Labor Research, 2
Updating of résumé, annual, 110
Upgrading of skills, 170

Verbal vocabulary, 181
Visualization
  of different profession, 127
  utilization of, 59–63
Vocabulary, 180–182
  and reading, 180

Wall Street Journal, 179
Weekends, as goal, career change and,
  126
What Color Is Your Parachute?, 179
Whiz kids, as vanishing breed, 19–20
Women, as CPAs, 190–91
Work
  hard, enjoyment of, entrepreneurship
    and, 144–45
  most important, at most productive
    time, 30
Workaholics, 71–72
Work habits
  change in, emotional problems and,
    16–17
  for lifetime, development of, 63–73
Work life, quality of, 9–13
Written vocabulary, 181

Year, review of previous, 112–15
Younger boss, coping with, 42–43